The
Golden Age
of
Islam

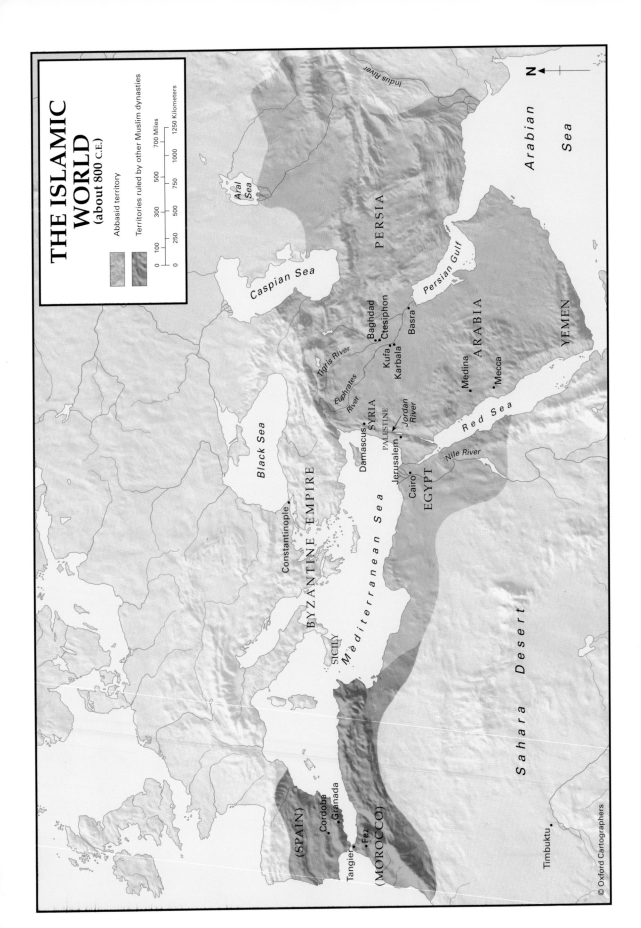

THE ISLAMIC WORLD
(about 800 C.E.)

Abbasid territory

Territories ruled by other Muslim dynasties

0   100   300   500   700 Miles

0   250   500   750   1000   1250 Kilometers

N

Indus River

Aral Sea

Caspian Sea

PERSIA

Persian Gulf

Baghdad
Ctesiphon
Basra

Tigris River

Kufa
Karbala

ARABIA

Euphrates River

Medina
Mecca

SYRIA

Black Sea

Damascus
PALESTINE
Jerusalem

Jordan River

Red Sea

YEMEN

Nile River

Arabian Sea

BYZANTINE EMPIRE

Constantinople

Cairo

EGYPT

Mediterranean Sea

SICILY

Sahara Desert

(SPAIN)
Cordoba
Granada

Fez

(MOROCCO)

Tangier

Timbuktu

© Oxford Cartographers

THE
GOLDEN AGE
OF
ISLAM

LINDA S. GEORGE

BENCHMARK BOOKS

MARSHALL CAVENDISH
NEW YORK

To Alexander
and the children of Baghdad

*G*rateful acknowledgment is made to Rochelle Kessler of the Department
of Asian Art at the Metropolitan Museum of Art, New York City,
for her generous assistance in reading the manuscript.

Benchmark Books
Marshall Cavendish Corporation
99 White Plains Road
Tarrytown, New York 10591-9001

© Marshall Cavendish Corporation 1998

LIBRARY OF CONGRESS CATALOGING-IN-PUBLICATION DATA
George, Linda S., date.
The golden age of Islam / Linda S. George.
p. cm. — (Cultures of the past)
Includes bibliographical references and index.
Summary: Covers the civilization of the Islamic Empire from the last years of the
eighth century to the thirteenth century.
ISBN 0-7614-0273-X (libr. binding)
1. Civilization, Islamic—Juvenile literature. [1. Civilization, Islamic. 2. Islamic Empire—History.]
I.Title. II. Series.
DS36.85.G47   1998   909'.097671—dc20   96-23806   CIP   AC

Printed in China

Photo research by Debbie Needleman

Front cover: Miniature of the archangel Gabriel, painted in Egypt or Syria in the 14th century
Back cover: Young Bedouin reading the Koran, Morocco

PHOTO CREDITS
Front cover and page 36: Copyright British Museum; page 6: The Louvre, Paris/Giraudon/Art Resource,
NY; page 7: Robert Frerck/Tony Stone Images; page 9: Bonhams, London/Bridgeman Art Library,
London; page 10, 33: Sonia Halliday Photographs; page 12, 44: Nabeel Turner/Tony Stone Images; page
15: Christie's Images/Bridgeman Art Library, London; page 17: Chester Beatty Library and Gallery of
Oriental Art, Dublin/Bridgeman/Art Resource, NY; page 20: British Library, London/Bridgeman Art
Library, London; page 22: Bibliotheque Nationale, Paris/Bridgeman/Art Resource, NY; page 24: Private
Collection/Bridgeman Art Library, London; page 26, 40, 53: Robert Frerck/Odyssey Productions/Chicago;
page 29: Book Arts Collection, Rare Book and Manuscript Library, Columbia University; page 31: The
Metropolitan Museum of Art, Cora Timken Burnett Collection of Persian miniatures and other art objects,
Bequest of Cora Timken Burnett, 1957 (57.51.21); page 34: National Library, Cairo/Giraudon/Art
Resource, NY; page 37: Sonia Halliday and Laura Lushington/Sonia Halliday Photographs; page 39: The
Metropolitan Museum of Art, Harris Brisbane Dick Fund, 1939 (39.20); page 42: Bodleian Library, Uni-
versity of Oxford, Ms. Ouseley (Add.24 f.55V); page 43: Musee D'Orsay, Paris/Lauros-Giraudon/Bridge-
man Art Library, London; page 47: The Metropolitan Museum of Art, Gift of J. Pierpont Morgan, 1917
(17.190.985); page 48: British Library, London/Bridgeman Art Library, London; page 54 and back cover:
Nicholas DeVore/Tony Stone Images; page 55, 71: Paul Chesley/Tony Stone Images; page 58: Hilarie
Kavanagh/Tony Stone Images; page 59: The Metropolitan Museum of Art, The Hagop Kevorkian Fund,
1970 (1970.170), photo by Schecter Lee; page 60: Paul Harris/Tony Stone Images; page 61: Institute of
Oriental Studies, St. Petersburg/Giraudon/Bridgeman Art Library, London; page 62: Rohan/Tony Stone
Images; page 63, 65: Scala/Art Resource, NY; page 64: Bibliotheque Nationale, Paris/Bridgeman Art
Library, London; page 67: Werner Forman/Art Resource, NY; page 68: Dave Bartruff; page 69: Musee
Paul Dupuy, Toulouse, France/Giraudon/Art Resource, NY; page 80: Marisa Escribano

Passages from the Koran which appear in Chapter Three are reprinted with the kind permission of
Simon & Schuster from *The Koran Interpreted*, translated by A. J. Arberry. Copyright 1955 by George
Allen & Unwin Ltd. The poem by Abu Nuwas, which appears on page 34, is reprinted with the kind
permission of the University of Texas Press from *An Introduction to Arab Poetics*, by Adonis, translated
from the Arabic by Catherine Cobham. Copyright 1985.

CONTENTS

CHAPTER ONE

A BEACON IN THE EAST

Around the year 800 C. E.* ambassadors of Charlemagne, then the mightiest ruler in all of Europe, made a visit to Baghdad, to the court of Harun al-Rashid. Harun ruled the great Muslim empire, which stretched from North Africa to the borders of India, an empire that covered more territory than even ancient Rome at its most powerful. Harun favored Charlemagne's ambassadors with gifts of opulent fabrics, costly perfumes, an intricate water clock, and an elephant.

Charlemagne, as king of the Franks, sought to make an alliance with Harun against their common enemy, the Byzantine Empire. Harun, for his part, hoped the Franks might assist him in subduing a rival Muslim dynasty in Spain, the Umayyads (oo-MY-yads).

Charlemagne represented in a bronze statue from the ninth or tenth century.

It is clear from medieval sources that Harun's empire was far more powerful and far more sophisticated than Charlemagne's. Harun's capital was a center of learning and supported the work of important scholars. Harun himself actively collected and studied the Greek manuscripts that preserved the science and philosophy of the classical period. While Charlemagne, too, recognized the importance of learning, he could barely read and never learned to write.

Harun ruled a great empire, an empire built on the religion of Islam, a religion that was not yet two hundred years old.

The Golden Age

In this book, we will explore a golden age that stretched from the last years of the eighth century—the time of Harun al-Rashid—to the middle of the thirteenth century C. E. During the time of Harun, Muslims controlled an expanse of territory from Spain to the borders of India. Harun ruled most

*Many systems of dating have been used by different cultures throughout history. This series of books uses B. C. E. (Before Common Era) and C. E. (Common Era) instead of B. C. (Before Christ) and A. D. (Anno Domini) out of respect for the diversity of the world's peoples.

of these lands, except for the western part of North Africa and Spain, which were held by other Muslim dynasties. Harun was the fifth ruler of the Abbasid (uh-BAS-id) dynasty. He ruled from Baghdad, in what is today Iraq, from 786 to 809 C. E. Abbasid political power did not last much past the time of Harun, and by the tenth century, his empire began to fall apart, breaking into many separately ruled domains. Meanwhile, though, Muslim civilization flourished.

Harun is a celebrated figure in Islamic history, not only for his military victories and his political power, but also because during his era the Islamic culture was taking shape. This great civilization matured during the age of the Abbasids, from the end of the eighth century to the middle of the thirteenth century. It flourished in Abbasid territory as well as in areas ruled by other Muslim dynasties. All across the Islamic world—from Cordoba in Spain, to Cairo in North Africa, to Damascus and Baghdad in the Middle East— philosophers and poets, artisans and merchants, were building this unique

In Spain, monuments remain of the great Muslim civilization that once flourished there. This is the famous Alhambra, a palace and fortress built in the thirteenth century, overlooking the city of Granada. The Alhambra, filled with astonishing carvings and mosaics, surrounded by magnificent gardens and fountains, inspired the Spanish saying, "There is nothing in life worse than being blind in Granada."

culture. What an exciting time it was! Students from Europe and from the far corners of the empire flocked to Islamic universities. Mathematicians introduced what we know as Arabic numerals and set out the principles of algebra. Physicians identified the causes and treatment of smallpox and other diseases and wrote the textbooks that would be used in Europe until well into the sixteenth century. From great observatories astronomers measured the earth and mapped the heavens. Important advances were made in many fields, advances that have shaped the world in which we live today.

The era of Abbasid glory came to a close when Baghdad was destroyed by the Mongols, a people from central Asia, in 1258 C. E. Even after the Mongols' conquest, though, intellectual and artistic activity continued in the Muslim world, and some of the most magnificent art and brilliant scholarship date from after the Mongol invasion. The Abbasids were by no means the last important Muslim rulers, nor did the end of the Abbasids mean decline in the civilization they helped define. Other great moments in Muslim civilization and political power were yet to come. It was during the age of the Abbasids, though, that Islamic civilization took its place as a world power and a great culture, one that was to leave a lasting mark on history.

Before Islam

The area around the Mediterranean Sea, as part of the Roman Empire before the coming of the Muslims, had enjoyed a high level of civilization and relative peace for many centuries. From the fourth century C. E., Constantinople—modern-day Istanbul, Turkey—replaced Rome as capital of the empire, and the center of power moved eastward. At the same time, the empire became Christian, although there remained communities of Jews and people who followed ancient religions. When the western half of the empire collapsed in the fifth century, the eastern half survived—and thrived—as the Byzantine Empire. (Byzantium was the old name of Constantinople.) In northern Europe and in Spain "barbarian" kings ruled.

To the east of the Byzantine Empire lay Persia, the empire of the Sasanids, encompassing modern-day Iraq and Iran and stretching into central Asia. This was an area of ancient cultures and cities. The official religion was Zoroastrianism, but the Sasanid Empire was an important center of Jewish religious teaching as well, and it included Christian communities and polytheistic Greeks.

The harsh life of the desert often fascinated Europeans. This painting of a Bedouin family was done in 1859 by Carl Haag, an English painter who lived for a time with a tribe in the Syrian desert.

The area that gave rise to Islam—the Arabian Peninsula north of Yemen—is for the most part desert, dotted with oases. Wandering Arab herders moved with their camels, sheep, and goats across the desert, while settled peoples lived in the oasis cities, tending crops and arranging for the sale of goods along ancient trade routes. The nomads—the Bedouin—and the settled people depended on each other, with the Bedouin guiding and protecting caravans of merchants and other travelers through their territories and the settled people providing food and other goods to the Bedouin. Various dialects of Arabic were spoken across this area.

In this sixteenth century miniature, Muhammad, with the angel at his side, preaches to some of the early converts to Islam. Muhammad's face is veiled, since many Muslims believe his face should not be represented.

The Rise of Islam

The religion of Islam appeared in the early years of the seventh century C. E., taken up first by the city dwellers of Mecca and Medina, then spreading to the Bedouin. Within decades its followers burst out of Arabia, thundering across North Africa and up into Europe and eastward over central Asia to the borders of China. How was it that the followers of this new religion could so quickly become such a powerful force?

A variety of factors account for the rise of Islam as a world power. Some features of the religion itself fueled this military whirlwind. Some features of the surrounding territories and their history also figured in the success of the Muslim armies.

Muhammad, the founder of Islam, known as the Prophet, was born about 570 C. E. in Mecca, a prosperous and cosmopolitan city. Mecca lies in a hot, barren valley near the crossroads of what were important north-south and east-west trade routes.

At the time of the Prophet, Mecca was a center of worship. The gods of the Arabs did not have human characteristics like the gods of the ancient Greeks. Their deities were represented by large standing stones and were worshipped in various shrines, the most important of which was the Kaaba in Mecca.

Muhammad taught that the worship of many gods was wrong and that people should believe in the one God—in Arabic, Allah—the God of the Jews and the Christians. Muhammad was to be the last in the line of prophets, which included Abraham, Moses, and Jesus, among others, sent by God to guide humankind. God's message given to Muhammad was to be the final word. Muhammad was therefore called the Seal of the Prophets.

Muhammad preached that people should submit themselves to the will of God. The word *Islam* means "submission" or "surrender." A Muslim is a person who surrenders to the will of God and tries to live according to the principles set down by God in the Muslim holy book, the Koran, and the principles exemplified in the life of Muhammad.

Muhammad's message was at first rejected by the powerful families of Mecca. Pilgrims visiting the Kaaba shrine in Mecca were an important source of income to these families. Perhaps the ruling families of Mecca also recognized that if they were to accept Muhammad's teachings, their own political power would be threatened.

The *Hijra*

Muhammad and his followers became less and less welcome in Mecca and in 622 they migrated to Medina, a city about two hundred miles to the north. Muhammad and his followers had been invited to Medina by its ruling families, who knew Muhammad to be a capable leader. They hoped he would be able to reconcile two warring tribes there. It is this event—the migration from Mecca, the *hijra* (HEJ-ra)—that Muslims take as the beginning of their calendar. Years in the Islamic calendar are counted from the year of the *hijra* and are written in English with the notation A. H., "*anno Hegirae*"—Latin for "in the year of the *hijra*."

From the beginning, Muhammad felt that the religion he preached should govern not only spiritual life but also political life. Followers of Islam should live in a state in which the law of the Koran was the law of the land. This idea was not new or surprising. At that time, much of the world was organized with religion and political power tightly bound together, as, for example, in Christian Byzantium.

In Medina Muhammad became not only the religious leader but also the political leader. Although he and his followers were now established in Medina, they looked to Mecca and the Kaaba as the most holy place of Islam. But still Mecca refused to accept Muhammad's teachings.

Modern worshippers circle the Kaaba, as part of their pilgrimage to Mecca. The Kaaba is the cubical building covered by a black cloth decorated with lines from the Koran embroidered with gold thread.

In the year 624 Muhammad's followers attacked a caravan returning to Mecca, striking at the lifeblood of that city. The two sides clashed in battle at Badr, near Medina. Three hundred Muslims, led by Muhammad, won victory over a thousand Meccans. This was Islam's first decisive military victory; the Muslims took it as evidence that God was on their side.

Still, it was not until 630 that Mecca came under Muhammad's authority. Muhammad made his triumphal return to Mecca in that year. Entering the Kaaba, the sanctuary used to worship the old deities, he smashed the ancient statues and declared, "Truth has come and falsehood has vanished."

Muhammad returned to Medina and continued to govern from there. After the new religion was accepted among the city dwellers of Mecca and Medina, the Bedouin also came to acknowledge Muhammad's authority. Some Bedouin tribes sent representatives to pay tribute—a kind of tax—to Muhammad; others had to be brought into the fold forcefully. In any case, those who converted to Islam paid *zakat*, a tax assessed on all believers. The *zakat* was used for the needs of the poor and also for more general state expenses such as support for those fighting "for the cause of God."

Another sort of tax, the *jizya* (JIZ-ya), or poll tax, was collected from non-Muslims, who were allowed to practice their own religions under the protection of Islam, in exchange for the payment of this tax. This, along with the *zakat*, helped fill the coffers of the growing Muslim empire and finance its conquests.

In 632, Muhammad led a pilgrimage to the holy city of Mecca for the final time. He returned to Medina and three months later took sick and died.

Muhammad's death led to a crisis because he had not designated a successor. By agreement of those close to Muhammad, Abu Bakr was chosen caliph (KAY-lif), or successor. He was an early convert and the highly respected father of Aisha (AAY-sha), one of Muhammad's wives. The issue of succession was to be the cause of much contention in later years and, finally, the basis for a major split among Muslims.

Early Conquests

In the years immediately following Muhammad's death, many of the Bedouin tribes that had agreed to pay the *zakat* to Muhammad had second thoughts about paying his successors. Some tribes tried to break away from Muslim authority, and a period of local wars followed. Soon, however, the tribes of the Arabian Peninsula, including those that had rebelled and some that had not previously recognized Muhammad, were brought under the authority of Islam.

The Bedouin were well suited to take up the sword of Islam. An important part of the life of these desert nomads was the raid. Tribes regularly raided one another, stealing livestock, their main source of wealth. These raids redistributed wealth in the harsh desert environment, where a tribe's livelihood could be wiped out by a well going dry or a lack of rain.

Once these Bedouin tribes accepted Islam, however, they were all supposed to be brothers. They could no longer attack one another. Instead,they banded together and turned their energies against their non-Muslim neighbors.

The neighbors, the Byzantine Empire to the north and the Sasanid

ARABS AND MUSLIMS

The word *Arab* originally referred to the people of the desert, the Bedouin, in contrast to the city dwellers. Both the Bedouin and the city dwellers of Arabia spoke Arabic, which was to become the sacred language of Islam, but the Bedouin were thought to speak the language in its purest form. City dwellers would often send their sons to live with the Bedouin for a time, as a sort of boarding school, to learn the ways of the desert.

In the early years of Islam, most of the Bedouin tribes converted to the new religion. They became the core of the armies. It was they who carried the banner of Islam and they who were identified in the conquered areas with the religion of Islam. Thus early on Arabs and Muslims came to be thought of as the same people. Later, as Islam spread and was taken up by diverse peoples, it was Arabic, the language of the Koran, that united them. Today Muslims around the world read the Koran in Arabic and say their prayers in Arabic. Muslims whose native language is not Arabic must learn it in order to perform their religious duties.

The word *Arab* as it is used today refers to people who speak Arabic, most of whom live in the area that stretches from Morocco to Iraq. Although Arabic is the language of the Koran, not all of the people who speak Arabic are Muslims. Many Arabs are Christians and some belong to other faiths. Arabs speak many different dialects of Arabic—just as Southerners in the United States speak an accented English different from that of people in Boston, and both speak differently from the British. While English speakers can usually understand one another,this is not always true for Arabic speakers. But even though a Moroccan may not be able to understand someone from Iraq, they share the same written language. The fact that Arabs share a written language has helped them preserve a common culture across a wide area and through many centuries.

A view of Damascus painted by a nineteenth century European artist.

Empire in Persia, to the east, were already torn apart and weakened by plagues and years of wars against each other. Their citizens were taxed heavily to finance the ongoing warfare. Meanwhile the Christian church was also in turmoil, with various groups breaking off from the established church. These groups, along with the Jews, were persecuted by the Byzantines.

The Seige of Damascus

Within a decade, Muslim armies had conquered the Sasanid Empire and plucked off some of the Byzantine Empire's choice provinces. To understand some of the factors contributing to this military whirlwind, we can look to the surrender of the city of Damascus in Syria. The Muslim army, under the leadership of Khalid ibn al-Walid (KHA-lid ib-nal-wa-LEED), surprised and defeated the Byzantine army near Damascus. Khalid laid siege to the city, and after six months, in September 635, Damascus surrendered.

Tradition has it that Khalid was aided by people within the walls of the city. Medieval Muslim historians recount many tales in which Christians or Jews inside cities under siege pointed out chinks in the wall or even actually opened the city gates to the Muslim conquerors.

Khalid ibn al-Walid sent this notice to the people of Damascus:

In the name of God, the compassionate, the merciful. This is what Khalid ibn al-Walid will grant to the inhabitants of Damascus if he enters their city: he promises them security for their lives, their property, and their churches. The walls of their city shall not be demolished, nor shall any Muslims be quartered in their houses. We offer the pact of God and the protection of his Prophet, the caliphs, and the believers. So long as they pay the jizya, *only good will come to them.*

After Damascus other cities and towns fell, one after the other. In one town people came out to greet the conquerors with singers and tambourine players. In another people said, "We like your rule and justice far better than the state of oppression and tyranny under which we have been living." Perhaps these Middle Eastern people welcomed the Muslims because they were Semites, too; they were of the same ethnic group as the Arabs and spoke languages related to Arabic.

Within a short time Muslim armies controlled most of Syria. Soon the city of Jerusalem in the Syrian province of Palestine fell. Muslim armies swept into Egypt and from there across North Africa. By the year 710 they had crossed into Spain.

Meanwhile, to the east, the Muslims pushed across the Euphrates River into Persia and in 637 marched on the Sasanid capital Ctesiphon (TES-i-fon), a city filled with riches beyond imagining. To the rough-edged Bedouin, the luxury they found there must have been overwhelming. Stories come to us of country-bumpkin soldiers trading gold pieces, uncommon in Arabia, for the more familiar but much less valuable silver.

The advance continued eastward and by 643 reached the border of India.

Arab tribespeople settled into the newly conquered territories, ready to take advantage of the economic opportunities there.

Arab Muslim rule in Persia was more precarious than in other areas of the Empire. The Persians and the Arabs belonged to different ethnic groups and spoke unrelated languages. Persian civilization went back more than a thousand years. Islamic rule took hold, however, and was to last. Over the next three centuries in Persia, Arabic became the official language and the language of cultivated society, but Persian culture never died out. It had a lasting influence on the literature and sciences that flourished in the Arabic language. The Persian language survived and is spoken in modern-day Iran, written with the Arabic alphabet.

Mosques, Muslim places of worship, follow the style of the first mosque, the Mosque of the Prophet Muhammad in Medina, depicted here in a 16th century watercolor. The mosque is the large enclosed area. Along its walls are minarets, or towers, from which believers are called to prayer.

Muhammad's Successors and the Caliphate

After Muhammad's death, Abu Bakr, now caliph, governed the Muslim community from Medina, living modestly and conducting the business of state from the courtyard of the Prophet's Mosque. This was a simple structure that Muhammad himself had helped build for communal worship and from which he, too, had governed. Abu Bakr ruled only two years, until his death in 634. Umar, another early convert and trusted adviser of the Prophet, followed him and ruled until 644.

Umar, like Abu Bakr, was related to the Prophet by marriage, his daughter Hafsa being one of Muhammad's wives. Umar was a man of great piety and virtue. He, too, lived a simple life and was said to have owned only one shirt and one robe, both of which were patched. Umar was killed by a slave in an act of personal vengeance. Uthman, his successor, ruled for twelve years and was killed in 656 during an uprising, setting the stage for a power struggle.

Ali, a cousin of the Prophet who was married to the Prophet's daughter Fatima (FAH-teh-muh), had supporters who argued from the beginning that he should succeed the Prophet. After the murder of Uthman, Ali became caliph, but his election was opposed by some, and war broke out. Ali struggled against the governor of Syria, Muawiya (mu-AH-we-a), but in 661 Ali was killed.

Muawiya, the first of the Umayyad caliphs, established his capital in Damascus, Syria. Under his rule the office of caliph came to be passed from father to son, succession no longer being determined by agreement of the community. The Umayyad dynasty ruled from 661 until 750.

The Sunni-Shiite Split

Ali was an important figure in early Islam who was to have lasting significance. His supporters believed that the caliph was also imam (i-MAHM), or religious leader, and that Ali was most qualified because of his direct links to the Prophet.

When Ali was killed, his supporters formed a political party, *shiat* Ali, "the party of Ali," or the Shiites (SHEE-ites). Their goal was to restore the caliphate to the descendants of Ali since they considered Ali's descendants to be the rightful successors to Muhammad.

The question of succession caused a major split among the believers, a division that has lasted to this day. On the one hand, there were those who accepted the four caliphs who followed Muhammad (Abu Bakr, Umar, Uthman, and Ali) and also the caliphs of the Umayyad and Abbasid dynasties. These came to be known as Sunni Muslims. Those who believed that only Ali and his descendants were the rightful successors are Shia Muslims, or Shiites.

The Coming of the Abbasids

Power was wrested from the Umayyads by the Abbasids, who traced their lineage back to Abbas, an uncle of the Prophet. The Abbasids destroyed the Umayyad dynasty and tried to kill every possible heir. The only one to escape was twenty-year-old Abd al-Rahman, who fled across North Africa and eventually established an Umayyad dynasty in Spain.

Meanwhile, the Abbasids moved their capital east into the area now known as Iraq. The second Abbasid caliph, al-Mansur, whose name means "the victorious," built the fabled city of Baghdad as his capital. Harun was the fifth of the Abbasid caliphs, known as al-Rashid, "the rightly guided one." The period of his rule became legendary, both in Europe and in the Muslim world, as a time of unprecedented splendor.

FATIMA, HER SONS, AND THE SHIITES

Fatima, born around 605, was one of the daughters of the Prophet and his first wife, Khadija (kha-DEE-ja). She married her cousin Ali, whom Muhammad had adopted and raised. She and Ali had two sons, Hasan and Hussein. Fatima, who was Muhammad's only child to survive him, herself died shortly after her father, in 633.

As the daughter of Muhammad and the mother of his only heirs, Fatima came to be venerated, especially among the Shiites, as the person through whom the Prophet's saintliness was passed on. When Ali was killed, they believed that the caliphate should then pass to Ali's eldest son, Hasan. Hasan was not interested in waging war to claim the caliphate; he renounced his claims to power and retired to Medina, where he died around 669.

Hussein, Ali's other son, later pressed his claims to the caliphate. In the year 680 he and his family and followers made their way to Iraq, the stronghold of his supporters, but were met at Karbala and slaughtered by the forces of the Umayyads. This battle is commemorated on the tenth day of the Muslim month of Muharram and is a day of mourning and sadness for the Shiites. Hussein's body was buried at Karbala (his head was sent to the caliph in Damascus), and his tomb remains a sacred place for Shiites.

CHAPTER TWO

LIFE IN THE GOLDEN AGE

Baghdad, the Royal Capital

By the time of Harun al-Rashid, Baghdad was already "a city with no equal in the world," in the words of an eleventh-century Arab historian. Harun's grandfather al-Mansur, "the Victorious," who ruled from 754 to 775, had built Baghdad on the Tigris, a river that would put his city in touch with lands as far away as China. Another major river, the Euphrates, flowed close by, connecting Baghdad to Syria and the lands beyond to the north and west. The surrounding countryside was watered by a system of canals, producing enough food to support a large city. Taxes to enrich the empire were collected from this prosperous farmland.

The official name al-Mansur gave his city was Medinat al-Salam, the "City of Peace." Baghdad, as the city came to be known, was the name of the village that had previously occupied this site. It means "given by God." Al-Mansur's capital was built as a round city about a mile and a half across, with high double brick walls dotted with towers, encircled by a deep moat. Along the outer walls were four

Even the caliph had to take a bath. The Prophet Muhammad said, "Cleanliness is part of the religion," and Muslims were steaming and scrubbing themselves while most Europeans feared and avoided baths.

The hammam, *or bath, was often luxurious and beautifully decorated with mosaics and geometric designs as in this picture. Here the caliph Harun al-Rashid is being scrubbed and shaved, while attendants wring out and dry the towels.*

equally spaced gates, each topped with a golden dome, from which radiated four highways leading to the four corners of the empire.

The city was a monument to the Abbasid Empire. The center of this empire—and of the world—was Baghdad, and in the exact center of Baghdad was the caliph. The area devoted to the caliph contained a large mosque and a palace covered with a great green dome topped with a statue of a horseman carrying a lance. Shops and living quarters for the people were built along the outer edges of the wall.

Medinat al-Salam did not last long as a perfectly round city. Even within the lifetime of al-Mansur, suburbs grew up outside the walls, and the round city was absorbed into the larger urban complex that became Baghdad.

Very quickly Persian taste and Persian ideas dominated. The Arabs, including royalty, intermarried with people of Persian stock; Persian songs and literature were sought after; and new government offices were created, based on Persian models.

Women in Abbasid Times

Khaizuran, Mother of Harun

The lives of women close to Harun give us a glimpse into intriguing dimensions of court life. Harun's mother, Khaizuran (khay-zu-RAN), was a powerful figure, even though she came to court as a slave, purchased by al-Mansur for his son, Harun's father. Despite her humble origins, she came to exert much behind-the-scenes control of the throne. Her determination to have things her way was such that she was even rumored to have had her son al-Hadi killed so that Harun, her favorite, could rule. (Al-Hadi ruled for only one year, before Harun.) Her two sons were the only sons named as heirs to their father's throne, even though Harun's father had had other sons by a wife of royal lineage.

An important feature of life under the Abbasids was slavery. Conquest had brought with it enormous wealth and contact with faraway places, two factors that encouraged and supported slavery. Slavery had been practiced since ancient times in the Middle East and was widespread in Byzantine and Persian territories. Islam put a special twist on the institution. First, Muslims were not permitted to enslave one another. Second, freeing a slave was a pious act that the Koran—the Muslim holy book—repeatedly urges believers to do.

Slaves, mainly from Africa and Central Asia, were bought and sold in markets such as this one in Yemen, pictured in a 13th century manuscript. At the top of the painting, the merchant weighs the coins the buyer has offered.

Although slaves were generally better off under Islam than in other societies, slavery was still a cruel institution. Some slaves were pressed into hard labor and lived in miserable conditions, leading to riots and uprisings. One such incident was the Zanj rebellion, in which thousands of black African—*Zanj* in Arabic—slaves brought to southern Iraq to drain the salt marshes, revolted. The rebellion began in 868, and it was not until 883 that the uprising was finally crushed by the Abbasids.

Slaves were obtained from various sources. Some were captured in battle. These could be ransomed and sent home. Others were purchased in slave markets, which flourished in the Arabian Peninsula, central Asia,

Europe, and Africa. Some especially desirable slaves were taught music, poetry, and other arts, and then sold for very high prices. Many young slave girls were educated in this way, and some grew to find favor with their masters, as Khaizuran did. The slave woman could be freed by her master, as Khaizuran was, and married.

A wealthy man—and certainly the caliph—might have hundreds of slave women, called concubines. They would keep him company and bear him children, who would be free. These women, along with his legal wives and their attendants, would make up his harem. The word *harem* comes from an Arabic root that means "forbidden or holy place," and it refers to the part of the house where the women live, an area forbidden to men outside the family.

Keeping women secluded in a separate part of the house, a custom borrowed from Persian aristocracy, was adopted by Islam during the Abbasid period. The practice had a long history. As early as the fourteenth century B. C. E., in the area between the Tigris and the Euphrates rivers, women of the royal household lived in separate quarters in the palace, and respectable women covered their heads and wore veils outside the home. By the seventh century C. E. most women in Byzantine and Sasanid cities were secluded and wore veils when they appeared in public. Poor city women and women who lived in the countryside often did not veil.

As we will see in Chapter Three, in the early days of Islam women led active lives at the center of society. In the time of Harun a woman like Khaizuran could still exercise a great deal of influence, and we read of women commanding troops in battle, composing poetry, and achieving renown as musicians. By the end of the tenth century, however, strict separation of men and women had become general throughout society.

Zubaida, wife of Harun

Harun's wife Zubaida (zu-BAY-da) was another illustrious figure of the age. Unlike Harun's mother, Zubaida was of royal blood and was, in fact, a cousin of the caliph. She was immensely wealthy in her own right and dispersed large sums for public works. Once, on pilgrimage to Mecca, Zubaida experienced firsthand that city's water shortage. As a result she financed an elaborate system of underground aqueducts to carry water to the city from a spring many miles away. For the comfort of pilgrims making their way from Kufa (in present-day Iraq) to Mecca, she had inns built along the road.

Zubaida was renowned for these and other pious works and also for

The eastern Mediterranean coastline and the coasts of the Arabian Peninsula produced sailors who were famous from ancient times. Under the Abbasid caliphs, seafaring merchants brought an amazing array of goods from faraway places to the markets of cities like Baghdad and Damascus.

her appreciation of luxury. It was said that her table was set with vessels of nothing less than gold and silver encrusted with gems. She dressed herself and her slave women in the most sumptuous of fabrics and she is said to have started a fad of wearing shoes decorated with jewels.

Aside from setting the fashion of the day and spending legendary sums of money, Zubaida wielded power in other ways. She no doubt played a role in having her son Muhammad declared heir to the throne, despite the fact that he was not Harun's firstborn. He did, in fact, succeed his father, taking the name al-Almin, "the Trustworthy," ruling from 809 to 813.

Everyday Life of the Ordinary People

In the ninth century Baghdad was the largest city the Middle East had ever seen and, indeed, it was the largest city in the world outside of China. It had a population of between 300,000 and 500,000 and had spread to both sides of the Tigris River, covering an area of about twenty-five square miles.

Beyond the royal household and its extravagances, how did ordinary people live? Although many were poor, and history tells us little about them, most people benefited from the high level of culture attained during the Golden Age. Goods from all over the empire and beyond were available in Baghdad: silks and porcelains from China; spices and dyes from India; precious stones, fabrics, and slaves from the lands of the Turks in central Asia; furs, honey, and slaves from Russia and Scandinavia; ivory, gold, and slaves from east Africa.

A home of the period would have had a large sitting room, furnished with a *diwan* (from which comes the English *divan*), a low couch extending around three sides of the room. The floors were covered with handwoven carpets strewn with cushions on which guests could sit. Food was served on large round trays set on low tables. While most people would use brass trays, in wealthy homes the trays would be made of silver. People sat down to meals of delicately spiced stews, fish served with lemon, all kinds of fruits and nuts, and other items that sound delectable even today.

Many sports familiar to us entertained people of ninth-century Baghdad. Horse races were major events. Polo, a game played on horseback, was adopted by the Arabs from the Persians. It was popular, as was a sort of hockey played with a ball and mallet. Royalty seemed to be particularly fond of hunting, and Harun's son al-Amin hunted lions. Hunting with falcons and hawks, a sport borrowed from Persia and popular in Harun's time, is still practiced today in some parts of the Arab world.

Indoors people amused themselves with pastimes such as backgammon and chess, both originally Indian games, which the Arabs learned from the Persians. Harun himself was an avid chess player and among the gifts he sent to Charlemagne was a chessboard. The game caught on in Europe, and

In this 13th century miniature painted for a Spanish ruler, two men play a game that looks very much like backgammon.

tradition has it that when the elephant Harun had sent to Charlemagne was killed in battle, its tusks were made into chess pieces, some of which have survived to this day.

A Passion for Learning

The high standard of living and the legendary opulence of this period went hand in hand with the flourishing of the arts and sciences. Islam's golden age was remarkable for its intellectual fervor.

IF YOU LIVED IN ABBASID TIMES

If you had been born in the golden age, your way of life would have been determined by the facts of your birth: whether you were a boy or a girl; wealthy or poor; free or slave; Muslim or non-Muslim. With this chart you can trace the course your life might have taken as a member of an upper-class Muslim family.

You were born in Baghdad . . . .

As a Boy . . .   **As a Girl . . .**

You live in a two-story house of mud brick. The front of the house, which looks onto a narrow street, is plain, except for the heavy wooden door decorated with beautiful carvings. Inside is a large open courtyard with a fountain. Two stairways lead to the second floor: one to the main hall, where guests are entertained, the other to the women's quarters.

At age 6 your formal schooling begins at the mosque, where you learn to read and write using the Koran as a textbook. You also study Arabic grammar, hadith (reported sayings or actions of Muhammad), arithmetic, and poetry. By the time you are 9 or 10, you have memorized the entire Koran, or at least major sections of it.

At age 12 you practice fencing, archery and horsemanship, necessary skills for a man. You may study at a mosque school or instead learn your father's business.

At age 20 you marry someone your family chooses. You spend your family time in the women's quarters with your wife and children. If you have more than one wife, you provide a separate apartment or house for each wife and her children. You entertain your guests in the main hall. You spend much of your time outside the home, at work or socializing at public entertainments.

At age 6 you begin your schooling at home with a private tutor. You learn to read and write from the Koran and you study hadith, polite literature and poetry. You learn household skills, such as spinning.

At age 12 your parents are planning your marriage. They have selected a husband for you, and you consent. The groom's family provides a dowry, part of which is paid to you at the marriage. You go to live with your husband, perhaps in a household with other members of his family.

As a wife and mother, you spend your days at home tending to your children and supervising your household. If you have inherited wealth, you invest it in a business or you use it to endow charities

If your husband dies or divorces you, you return to your father or you live with one of your grown children. If your husband dies, you inherit a share of his estate. If your husband divorces you, he pays you the remainder of your dowry.

When you die, your body is washed and wrapped in a plain white cloth. You are buried with your face turned toward Mecca. Members of your family, especially the women, visit your grave on certain festivals.

Islam teaches that learning is a duty of the believer. The Prophet himself enjoined the faithful to "seek knowledge, even if it takes you to China." "The ink of scholars is more precious than the blood of martyrs" is another saying attributed to the Prophet.

When Muslims found themselves masters of cities that had long traditions of carefully cultivated arts and sciences, they saw that they had much to learn. The genius of Islamic civilization is that it was open to the learning and traditions of the cultures it had conquered. It studied them and built upon them.

Classical Learning Passes into Arabic

Harun himself had an intense intellectual curiosity and on his raids into Byzantine-held territories, he sought out Greek manuscripts, such as the works of Aristotle and Euclid. His successors were equally zealous collectors. In order to be of use, though, the texts they acquired had to be translated into Arabic. For this the Arabs relied on the skills of those within their realm who knew Greek—mainly Jews and Christians.

Major translation projects were begun under the second Abbasid caliph, al-Mansur, and work continued through the time of Harun and beyond. Harun's son al-Mamun, who succeeded Harun's son al-Amin, founded at Baghdad in 830 the Bayt al-Hikma, the "House of Wisdom." This institution contained, along with a translation department, a library and a school. The Bayt al-Hikma was one of the most important educational institutions of its time.

One of the major figures who worked at Bayt al-Hikma was Hunayn ibn Ishaq (809–873), a Christian. Hunayn and his school were responsible for translating into Arabic works of Aristotle, Plato's *Republic*, and a wide range of classical medical texts. Some of these works have been lost in the original Greek and survive only in the Arabic translations. Hunayn's skill was so highly valued that al-Mamun paid him the weight in gold of the books he translated.

Translating the works of classical Greek thought required refining the Arabic language and coining new words to express the most precise scientific and philosophical concepts. By the tenth century Arabic had become the language of scholarship as well as the language of diplomacy and polite culture from central Asia all the way to Spain. Through much of the Middle

THE ARABIAN NIGHTS

The Arabian Nights, or *The Thousand and One Nights*, is a collection of fantastic tales that were popular in the medieval Arabic-speaking world. The tales are full of genies, magic, and amazing characters—princesses who battle demons, slave girls, wise men, foolish princes, and talking animals.

The stories in the collection are all told by the fictional Shahrazad to the king Shahriyar. Shahriyar's first queen betrayed him by taking up with another man, and he vows that no woman will ever again deceive him. To ensure this, he takes a bride for only one day, then has her killed the next morning. All of the unmarried women in the kingdom are terrified of being forced to marry the king and then being killed. Brave and clever Shahrazad, though, goes to offer herself to the angry king. As the night wears on and the hour of her death approaches, Shahrazad begins to tell a story. The king is so intrigued that he spares her life so that she might finish the story the next night. Shahrazad tells story after story, and Shahriyar comes to love not only the stories but also Shahrazad. Her life—and the kingdom—is saved.

The outline of the story of Shahriyar and Shahrazad is Persian, and some of the stories, particularly the animal fables, appear to be Indian. The core stories were borrowed into Arabic sometime before the ninth century C. E. and grew from there. Stories were added and the collection came to include characters such as the caliph Harun al-Rashid and his companion Jafar, who go about the streets of Baghdad in disguise, eavesdropping on the lives of ordinary people. Later additions include "The Seven Voyages of Sindbad the Sailor," "Aladdin and His Magic Lamp," and "Ali Baba and the Forty Thieves."

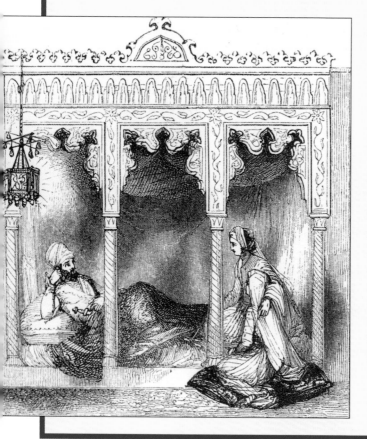

The Thousand and One Nights was never regarded as important literature in the Arabic-speaking world. The stories were simply popular entertainment composed by anonymous storytellers. In the Western world, though, the stories took on a life of their own. In the early eighteenth century Antoine Galland, a Frenchman, learned of the stories and translated them, along with some new ones he had heard, into French. Galland's tales were enormously popular and were soon translated into English. A sort of Arab craze began in Europe, with writers imitating the "Arab tale" and "oriental" style becoming the rage in fashion and art. The stories have been told and retold in every possible form, from scholarly editions to cartoons and bedtime stories.

Shahrazad tells one of her stories to the king.

Ages, Arabic was an important language of learning, even in Europe.

In the pages that follow we will refer to "Arabic sciences" and "Arabic arts" rather than "Muslim sciences and arts." The scholars whose works we will read about were not all Muslims. Some were Christians, Jews, or worshipers of many deities. They came from all parts of the Muslim empire: from Persia, India, central Asia, North Africa, and Spain. The connecting thread is that they all wrote in Arabic.

Arabic Sciences

Medicine

Hunayn ibn Ishaq and his colleagues translated into Arabic all the major classical texts on medicine—including the works of Hippocrates, Dioscorides, and Galen—and the writings of the Byzantine physicians of the seventh century. Hunayn, who had studied medicine with a famous Persian physician, himself wrote an introduction to medicine, summarizing the classical works.

To understand the process of how the Arabs added to and transformed the classical texts, we can look at the work of Dioscorides (die-us-KOR-uh-deez), a Greek physician and pharmacologist who died about 90 C. E. His famous book *De materia medica*, "On Medical Materials," details ways in which many plants, animal products, and minerals could be used as medicines.

The Arabic "translations" of Dioscorides expanded greatly on the original work. Dioscorides' work contained reference to about six hundred plants. The oldest extant Arabic manuscript contains descriptions and uses for fifteen hundred plants, adding items that were perhaps unknown to Dioscorides.

After the period of translation, several important original medical texts were produced, mainly by Persian physicians who wrote in Arabic. One of the most illustrious of these was al-Razi, chief physician at the hospital in Baghdad, who lived from 865 to 925. Known in the West as Rhazes, he was an original thinker and prolific author, credited with more than one hundred major works. His *Book of Secrets*, which was translated into Latin in the twelfth century, remained the chief source of knowledge about chemistry in Europe for two hundred years.

Al-Razi is known for his work on smallpox and measles. In his book on this subject, he taught how to diagnose smallpox, how to treat it, what caused it, how to keep it from spreading, and how to distinguish it from

This page from Dioscorides' De materia medica *describes how to prepare a medicine made from honey, as the pharmacist in the illustration is doing. The page comes from a copy of the book made in Baghdad in the 13th century.*

measles. In another work al-Razi discussed psychiatric medicine with insights still valid today. Al-Razi's medical encyclopedia was translated into Latin in 1279 by a Jewish physician in Sicily and was printed and reprinted many times, well into the sixteenth century. The work strongly influenced medicine as it developed in the Western world.

The first hospital in the Muslim world was opened in Baghdad during the rule of Harun, and soon other hospitals were built in Baghdad and in other parts of the empire. During Abbasid times physicians and pharmacists had to pass tests in order to be licensed.

Astronomy

The science of astronomy flourished under Islam. As in other areas, the Arabs sought out and translated many texts left by the Greeks, the Persians, and the Indians. The work of the famous Alexandrian astronomer Ptolemy, who flourished from around 127 to 145 C. E., was the main source for Greek astronomy. Ptolemy's major work, which takes the earth as the center of the universe, is known to this day by its Arabic title, *Almagest.*

Astronomy was particularly important to Muslims, and for very practical reasons. As Islam spread as far as the Atlantic coast of North Africa, into Spain, and to the east as far as China, praying in the direction of Mecca, as Muslims are required to do, became no simple matter. One cannot face east (or west) and assume one is facing Mecca. Complicated calculations of latitude and longitude, based on concepts of spherical trigonometry, are necessary. The mathematics upon which these calculations are based were formulated in the Golden Age. In the fourteenth-century an ambitious astronomer performed these calculations for hundreds of positions scattered all across the earth's surface. This was clearly an intellectual exercise, since it was unlikely that a Muslim in the fourteenth century would need to find the direction of Mecca from the North Pole. The numbers were recently checked by computer and found to be very close to modern results.

Muslims are to pray five times a day, at times set according to the sun's position in the sky. With enthusiasm Muslim astronomers took up the challenge of determining precise times for prayer, utilizing advanced mathematics and an understanding of the rotation of the earth.

While astronomy could help the earnest believer in the practice of the faith, the study was carried well beyond religious uses. The caliph al-Mamun built an observatory at Baghdad and a second one outside Damascus. From these places his astronomers checked and, when necessary, corrected the data given in Ptolemy's *Almagest,* including the length of the solar year and the calculation of when the equinoxes occur. Other Arab astronomers added to

At this observatory in 16th century Istanbul, astronomers were equipped with the most sophisticated instruments, some of which had been used by Muslim astronomers for centuries. Note the globe. One of the astronomers peers through a sextant, another charts something—perhaps the orbit of a planet—with a compass, and one holds an astrolabe, a disk-like instrument first used by the ancient Greeks.

Poetry in the Golden Age

Poetry has always been a highly valued art in the Arabic-speaking world, and the golden age produced many poets whose words are memorized and appreciated to this day. Abu Nuwas (ah-boo-noo-WAHS) was a special favorite of Harun al-Rashid and one of the great poets of his time. Here Abu Nuwas gives a glimpse into the mind of the poet:

But I say what comes to me
From my inner thoughts
Denying my eyes.
I begin to compose something
In a single phrase
With many meanings,
Standing in illusion,
So that when I go towards it
I go blindly,
As if I am pursuing the beauty
   of something
Before me but unclear.

A ruler surrounded by poets, musicians, and singers. From The Book of Songs, *a collection of Arabic poetry compiled in the tenth century.*

A particularly colorful poet was Wallada bint al-Mustakfi (WAH-lah-da bint al-mos-TAK-fee), who lived from 1001 to 1080. She was the daughter of the caliph of Cordoba, in Islamic Spain. Her mother is thought to have been an Ethiopian Christian slave. Wallada was a witty and cultivated woman who lived an independent life. She did not marry, she did not wear a veil, and she opened her home to poets, artists, and intellectuals. Among those who visited her was Ibn Zaydun, one of the greatest poets of Arab Spain, who fell madly in love with her. Their feelings for one another inspired each of them to compose many verses. Following are some lines by Wallada:

Wait for my visit until darkness falls,
For I know that night is the best guardian of secrets.
If the sun felt what I feel for you,
It would not shine.
If the moon felt it,
It would not appear in the sky.
And if the stars felt it,
They would cease their motion.

The love poetry of Islamic Spain was famous for its beauty and delicacy. It was known in the south of France and very likely influenced the love songs of the troubadours.

Ptolemy's tables and revised some of his computations of the orbits of the moon and the planets. Arab astronomical tables charting the movements of the planets and the stars eventually replaced the Greek and Indian tables and came to be used even in China. Many star names we use today come from the Arabic.

Al-Mamun's astronomers also undertook measurements to determine the circumference of the earth, checking figures derived by the ancient Greeks. Clearly al-Mamun's astronomers (and the ancient Greeks) knew that the earth was round. The Arab calculation was very close to modern measurements.

Mathematics

Important advances in mathematics went hand in hand with advances in astronomy; in fact, many of the important astronomers were also mathematicians. One of the most influential figures was al-Khwarizmi (al-kwa-RIZ-mee), who lived from about 780 to 850. He participated in the measurement of the earth's circumference mentioned above, and he compiled tables of the movements of the stars and planets. He was responsible for the first map of the heavens and the earth produced in the Muslim world, and his geography continued to be used until the fourteenth century. His contributions to mathematics were equally impressive. His book on algebra, *al-jabr* in Arabic, was translated into Latin in the twelfth century and remained the principal mathematics text used in European universities until the sixteenth century. Al-Khwarizmi's name gives us the word *algorithm*.

Al-Khwarizmi's work introduced the West to what we know as Arabic numbers. These numbers are known in Arabic as *hindi*, since they were brought to al-Mansur's court by a Hindu scholar. That Hindu scholar also introduced the notion of zero, which passed into Arabic mathematics and from there into Europe.

Breakthroughs were made in many other fields during this Golden Age: in optics (the study of light and how the eye sees it), in physics, in physiology, in engineering, as well as in philosophy and the arts. Some of the poetry and prose produced during this era are still regarded as among the best works ever written in Arabic.

CHAPTER THREE

ISLAM

A central belief of Islam is that the Koran—the Muslim holy book—is the word of God, revealed to Muhammad through the archangel Gabriel. The word *Koran* means "reading" or "recitation."

When Muhammad was about forty, he began to have religious visions and would retreat to a cave outside Mecca to contemplate these visions in solitude. On one of these retreats, one night toward the end of the month of Ramadan, an angel came to him in the form of a man. "Recite," the angel said.

"But I am not a reciter," Muhammad replied. "Recite," the angel repeated. Again Muhammad replied, "But I am not a reciter." The third time the angel said:

> Recite: In the name of thy Lord who created,
> created Man of a blood-clot.
> Recite: And thy Lord is the Most Generous,
> who taught by the Pen,
> taught Man that he knew not.
> —Sura 96: 2–6, *The Holy Koran*

This was the first of the revelations to Muhammad. The language of the Koran is powerful and eloquent, and Muslims take it as a miracle that Muhammad, who was an unschooled man, one who was not a "reciter," spoke these words.

"Recite!" the angel said to Muhammad. This miniature of the archangel Gabriel was painted in Egypt or Syria in the fourteenth century.

The Prophet Abraham

The story of the prophet Abraham—Ibrahim in Arabic—is important in Islam. It establishes where the Muslims came from, it explains some central rituals, and it relates Islam to Judaism and Christianity.

The book of Genesis in the Hebrew Bible

recounts the story of Abraham. God told Abraham that from him would come a people as numerous as the stars. But at the time Abraham had no children. He was a man of eighty-five, and his wife, Sarah, was seventy-six. It seemed unlikely that they would have children. Sarah gave Abraham her handmaid Hagar, an Egyptian woman, in the hope that Hagar might bear him a child. And she did. A son was born to Hagar, and he was named Ishmael, in Arabic Ismail (is-ma-EEL).

Years passed, the boy grew, and God spoke again to Abraham. By now Abraham was one hundred and Sarah ninety. God told Abraham that Sarah would bear him a son, who would be called Isaac. After Isaac was born, Sarah insisted that Hagar and Ishmael leave. Abraham sent them away reluctantly, but God assured him that Ishmael would be blessed.

Abraham is here depicted in a stained glass window at Canterbury Cathedral in England, built in the twelfth century. Both Jews and Muslims look to Abraham as their spiritual father.

Hagar and Ishmael left Abraham's house and traveled to a barren valley. They were alone and had no water. Hagar became frantic that Ishmael would die of thirst. The book of Genesis tells us that the angel of God said to her, "Arise, lift up the lad, and hold him in thine hand; for I will make him a great nation." (Genesis 21:18) Then God showed Hagar a well, and she gave the boy water.

This story is retold in the Koran. The "great nation" that sprang from Ishmael was the Arabs. Many centuries later, it was the Arabs to whom the religion of Islam was revealed and they who became the first Muslims. Thus Muslims trace their spiritual heritage back to Abraham. The Jews also trace their spiritual heritage back to Abraham, but through his other son, Isaac.

The story of Ishmael continues with Abraham visiting him and his mother in the holy place to which God had led them. The Koran relates that Abraham helped Ishmael build a sanctuary in this holy place for worship of the one God. They built this sanctuary near the well of Zamzam, the well the angel had opened for Hagar. This sanctuary was the Kaaba, the square building in Mecca that became the focal point of Islam.

The word *Islam* comes from an Arabic root that means "submission" or "surrender." This word appears in the Koran in connection with Abraham and Ishmael, who provide an example of how the believer is to submit to the will of God. In the Koran Abraham tells his son that he has dreamed that he would have to sacrifice him. "Father, do as you are commanded," Ishmael replies. Both are prepared to submit to God's will, but God intervenes and the boy is ransomed by the sacrifice of a ram. It is Abraham's submission to God's will—even to the point of sacrificing his own son—that marks him as a true believer. The Bible recounts a similar incident concerning Abraham and his son Isaac.

The idea that the Arabs descended from Ishmael was widely held even before Muhammad. Flavius Josephus, the famous Jewish historian of the first century C. E., wrote of Ishmael as "the founder of their [the Arabs'] race." A Christian historian writing in the fifth century explained that the Arabs shared some customs with the Jews—such as not eating pork—because of their connection with the Jews through Abraham.

The Five Pillars of Islam

The religion taught by Muhammad held believers to five basic duties. These five duties are the Pillars of Islam.

The First Pillar: *Shahada* (Testimony)

Shahada (sha-HAD-a) means giving testimony or making the statement of belief. It means saying the words "I testify that there is no god but the one God and Muhammad is the Prophet of God." A person who utters these words is considered a Muslim, and no one can question his or her belief.

The Second Pillar: *Salat* (Prayer)

Muslims are to pray five times a day facing Mecca. Prayers may be said individually or with the congregation in the mosque. The Friday midday prayer is the major communal prayer, the time when the congregation comes together in the mosque.

Islam teaches that everyone is equal in the sight of God. In the mosque men line up together, shoulder to shoulder, rich man next to poor man. No one can expect a special place in the mosque because of his position or wealth. All are equal before God.

Women often pray at home, but they may come to the mosque. They

This elaborately decorated mihrab, *or prayer niche, once stood in a mosque. The* mihrab *is built into the wall to show believers the direction of Mecca. The calligraphy in the rectangle in the middle of the niche says, "The mosque is the home of every religious person." The calligraphy on the white background outlining the niche tells of the five Pillars of Islam, the duties of the faithful. On the outer border are lines from the Koran describing the rewards in heaven that will come to dutiful believers.*

In Fez, Morocco, at a mosque built in the ninth century, men wash before prayer.

worship in a separate area of the building, just as women do in orthodox Judaism and in some Christian sects.

Prayer is a time of remembering and thinking of God. To prepare for prayer, the believer must be pure and clean, in mind and body. To cleanse the body, the believer must wash his or her face, hands, arms, and feet. Mosques have a fountain in the outer courtyard for this washing.

The prayers are verses from the Koran praising God and they are accompanied by bowing the head, bending, and kneeling with the forehead to the ground. The entire congregation says the prayers together and performs the bending and kneeling in unison. If one is praying alone, one would say the same verses and bow and bend and kneel in the same way.

The Third Pillar: *Zakat* (Giving)

The Koran teaches generosity. All things belong to God. Human beings are to use wisely what God has given them and to share with others less fortunate. Muslims share with others by paying the *zakat*, an obligatory contribution calculated at 2-1/2 percent of one's wealth. The money goes to the needy and for other causes that benefit the community as a whole.

The word *zakat* means both "to grow" and "to purify." By giving a portion of his or her wealth for the good of the community, the believer purifies the wealth and, as when pruning a plant, encourages new growth. One may give more than the required 2-1/2 percent; giving secretly, without recognition, is encouraged. In addition to the required contribution, alms are given on certain holidays, such as Ramadan.

The Fourth Pillar: *Sawm* (The Fast)

Muslims must fast for the month of Ramadan, the ninth month of the Islamic calendar, the month during which the Koran was first revealed to Muhammad. During this month, from sunrise to sunset, Muslims eat nothing and drink nothing, not even water. People who are sick, elderly, or on a journey, and women who are pregnant or nursing a child, are excused, but they must make up the number of days missed at a later time. People who are physically unable to fast at all should feed a needy person for every day missed. Children usually begin to fast when they reach the age of twelve, but some begin earlier.

Observance of the fast is another way in which believers come together as a community and as equals. All across the world Muslims fast during the month of Ramadan, rich and poor, old and young, men and women. Fasting reminds the rich person what it is to be hungry, and it encourages him or her to be generous. Fasting purifies the body, and the pangs of hunger remind one to think of God all day long.

The end of Ramadan is marked by a feast, Eid al-Fitr, one of the principal holidays in the Muslim calendar. It is celebrated by visiting family and friends, sharing meals, and giving special gifts to the poor.

SUFISM AND THE MYSTIC RABIA

Sufis are the mystics of Islam. The name is thought to come from the word *suf*, which means wool, the rough cloth these believers wore, symbolic of their preference for a life of simplicity over one of luxury. Sufis seek unity with God through various forms of meditation and contemplation of God and divine love. To be open for communion with God, they remove themselves from earthly concerns, often adopting a life of poverty and solitude.

Although the veneration of saints is frowned upon in orthodox Islam, many Sufis are remembered for their piety and are regarded as saints. Among these are many women, most prominent of whom is Rabia (ra-BEE-a), who lived from 717 to 801. The earliest written accounts of her life date from nearly two hundred years after her death, and by this time much was already legend.

Rabia was born in Basra, in what is now Iraq, probably of a poor family. She was orphaned and sold into slavery. One night her master came upon her praying and saw a light around her head, illuminating the entire house. He recognized something holy about her and freed her the next morning. She left his house, following her call to the contemplation of God.

Many miracles are attributed to Rabia. Once on the pilgrimage to Mecca, the ass which was carrying her baggage died while the pilgrims were still deep in the desert. The others with whom she was traveling offered to take her and her things with them, but she would not accept their offer. She would trust God to take care of her. Alone in the desert, she prayed, and had hardly finished before the ass stood up, alive again, and they went on their way. Another account tells of how, when she was again on the road to Mecca, the Kaaba left its place in Mecca and miraculously appeared before her.

A Sufi teacher preaches to an attentive audience in a mosque. The older men sit closest to the teacher, and behind them are the younger men. The women, most of whom are veiled, sit in a separate section of the mosque where they listen to the preacher and tend to their children.

The Fifth Pillar: Hajj (Pilgrimage)

The fifth duty of a Muslim is to make the pilgrimage to Mecca at least once in his or her lifetime if possible. Like other Muslim rituals, this one symbolizes the equality of believers before God and reinforces a sense of community. During the Month of the Hajj, believers from all over the world gather in Mecca.

The pilgrim begins his or her hajj by leaving the trappings of earthly life behind and putting on a plain, white, seamless garment. Pilgrims from many lands and many cultures, all dressed in simple, white garments enter the Great Mosque and circle the Kaaba seven times. The pilgrim should kiss the Black Stone or at least touch it. The Black Stone, embedded in the Kaaba, is the celestial stone believed to have been brought to Abraham by an angel.

Beginning in medieval times, great caravans of pilgrims bound for Mecca would set out every year from Yemen, Iraq, Syria and Egypt, each led by a splendidly outfitted camel bearing a beautiful Koran and a magnificent carpet to be placed at the tomb of the Prophet in Medina. This painting was done in the 19th century by a French artist.

Worshippers pray at the Great Mosque in Mecca. At the center is the Kaaba, the cubical building draped in black.

The pilgrim prays at the place where Abraham stood and drinks from the well of Zamzam, which was opened by the angel for Ishmael.

Other rituals included in the hajj reenact parts of the story of Abraham and Ishmael. The pilgrimage ends with the sacrifice of a sheep, commemorating Abraham's sacrifice of a ram in place of Ishmael. This is Eid al-Adha, "the feast of sacrifice," a major celebration throughout the Islamic world.

Jihad (Struggle)

Some Muslims consider *jihad* (je-HAD), or struggle, to be the sixth pillar of Islam. One of the meanings of *jihad* is personal struggle—the effort and work required to be the best Muslim one can be. It is the struggle against evil.

Jihad also relates to the duty of Muslims to invite others to Islam. The Koran calls this "the great jihad": "So obey not the unbelievers, but struggle with them thereby mightily." (25:53) This great struggle is fought with the

Koran, not with the sword. The Koran makes it very clear that Islam should not be forced on others: "No compulsion is there in religion." (2:257)

Jihad is also translated "holy war." Believers must fight to defend Islam. If one fights and is killed in the cause of Islam, he or she becomes a *shahid* (sha-HEED), or martyr, and goes directly to Paradise. Some Muslims believe that they must live in a country governed by Islamic law and therefore should fight for the establishment of that law. Others believe that they must fight to defend their religion only if Islam is attacked or if they are not being allowed to fully practice their religion. Being able to fully practice their religion may mean having access to holy places, being allowed to dress according to religious beliefs, or even being able to control the kinds of literature and entertainment available to everyone.

Clearly, believers differ greatly in what they understand as an attack on Islam and on when they feel that defense is necessary. Believers also differ on what they consider defense and in what circumstances they can justify violence. Just as in Christianity, Judaism, and other religions, some believers at various times in history—and even today—have used violence in the name of religion.

The Koran

The Koran is the collection of God's words revealed to Muhammad through the archangel Gabriel. Muhammad did not himself write down the words revealed to him, but he oversaw the work of scribes who began this task. By the time of Muhammad's death, the entire text had not yet been recorded. The words, though, were preserved in the memory of believers and passed on as spoken words. To us that may seem an astonishing feat—the text is as long as the New Testament—but in the seventh century people were used to memorizing lengthy texts. Although the Arabs had a written language at this time, they also had a strong oral tradition, that is, a habit of preserving texts— poems, for example—in spoken, not written form.

The caliph Abu Bakr, who succeeded Muhammad as leader of the Muslim community, began efforts to put together a complete written text, and the task was finished under the third caliph, Uthman.

The Koran is made up of 114 *suwar* (singular, *sura*), or chapters, and is arranged with the longest chapters first. The longest chapter is 286 verses and the shortest is 3. The entire text is preceded by the opening prayer, the *fatiha*

(FAA-ti-ha), which has only 7 verses. Any recitation of text from the Koran is always introduced by the words, "God said."

The Koran tells of many figures familiar in Jewish and Christian traditions. The story of creation and of Adam and Eve's fall from grace are recounted, as are the stories of Noah, Abraham, Ishmael, Joseph, Moses, Solomon, Job, and Jonah, among others. An entire chapter is entitled "Mary," and in it she is described as the purest of women. In the Koran Jesus is born miraculously, without a human father. Although miracles are attributed to Jesus, he is not regarded as the Son of God, but simply as one of the prophets. The Koran also lays out regulations Muslims are to follow with respect to diet, prayer, fasting, pilgrimage, alms giving, marriage, divorce, inheritance, and other aspects of social life and individual duty. The worst sin and the only unpardonable one is that of worshipping other gods.

The Koran describes God in his majesty and power:

> God
> there is no god but He, the
> Living, the Everlasting.
> Slumber seizes Him not, neither sleep;
> to Him belongs
> all that is in the heavens and the earth. . . .
> His Throne comprises the heavens and earth;
> the preserving of them oppresses Him not;
> He is the All-high, the All-glorious.
> —Sura 2: 256, *The Holy Koran*

Judgment Day is frightful: "when the stars shall be extinguished, when heaven shall be split, when the mountains shall be scattered . . ." (Sura 77: 9–11) The dead are awakened and they stand shoulder to shoulder across a desolate plain, waiting as their deeds are weighed and their souls judged. People will have to answer for their actions. Did they help the poor and orphaned or did they care only for themselves? Those who are saved go to Paradise, depicted as a beautiful garden with flowing rivers and fountains, shaded by fruit trees, where the air is fragrant with musk and camphor. There the saved are surrounded by loved ones and wonderful food and drink. Most important of all, Paradise is the abode of God.

Hell is the place of fire, of agonizing solitude, and of eternal regret.

"God is the light of the heavens and the earth." Decorated with lines from the Koran, the lamp itself becomes a symbol of God's light. This lamp hung in a mosque built in Cairo in the thirteenth century.

Hadith

Believers look to other religious texts as well to help them understand the meaning of the Koran. Most important of these is the record of what Muhammad said and did, preserved in a body of texts called the hadith, or "narratives." These are stories recounted by the Companions of the Prophet—people who actually knew him. What Muhammad said or did in a particular situation provides the example for how believers should act.

The hadith, like the Koran, were at first transmitted from person to person by word of mouth. It was not until the middle of the ninth century that they were written down.

Hadith cover everything from good manners to proper burial practices. In the following hadith, the Prophet instructed his followers on how to eat so that guests would feel comfortable and not go away hungry:

Ibn Umar said that the Messenger of God—peace and blessings of God be upon him—said: "When food is placed before guests, no one should

In this 16th century Persian miniature, Muhammad is shown on his miraculous journey to heaven. According to tradition, Muhammad was carried from Mecca one night, on the legendary horse Buraq, to the Jewish temple in Jerusalem, and from there was taken up through the seven heavens into the presence of God. Muhammad's face is veiled, since many Muslims believe his face should not be represented by artists.

get up until the food is removed, nor should anyone take his hand away from the food until everyone is finished. If one person takes his hand from the food, his companions may feel embarrassed to continue eating, and they may stop, even though they are still hungry."

Another hadith urges believers to share their meals with others:

Umar said that the Messenger of God—peace and blessings of God be upon him—said: "Eat together and do not eat alone, because the blessing is with company."

Believers should help one another to behave properly:

Anas said that the Messenger of God—peace and blessings of God be upon him—said: "Help your brother, whether he is the wrongdoer or the one to whom wrong is done."

His companions said, "Oh Messenger of God, we understand helping the one who is wronged, but how do we help the wrongdoer?"

He said, "Take hold of his hands and keep him from doing wrong."

Slaves should be treated kindly:

Abu Dharr said . . . . the Prophet—peace and blessings of God be upon him—said to me: Your slaves are your brothers. God has placed them under your control. When you have others under your control you should feed them what you eat, clothe them with your own clothes, and not ask them to do more than they can. And if you ask them to do a difficult task, you should help them do it.

Sharia, or Islamic Law

The Sharia (sha-REE-a) is the body of laws that govern the community of believers. Sharia addresses many aspects of life, including marriage, divorce, inheritance, certain points of criminal law, and some areas of commercial law. Islamic law was administered by judges appointed by the rulers. When necessary, judges would refer complex questions to legal experts for a ruling.

The Life of Muhammad

Muhammad was born into the Quraysh tribe, which was the most powerful tribe in Mecca. His father had died before he was born, and his mother died when he was six, leaving Muhammad to be raised by his uncle, Abu Talib. Because Muhammad had a reputation for being intelligent and trustworthy, he came to the attention of Khadija, a wealthy merchant. She employed him to lead her caravan.

Khadija soon asked Muhammad to marry her, and he agreed. She was a widow who had been married twice and had several children. At the time of her marriage to Muhammad, she was forty and he twenty-five.

Khadija and Muhammad had four daughters: Zaynab, Ruqayya, Fatima, and Umm Kulthum. Muhammad also adopted his cousin Ali, who was then about five years old. Ali's father, Abu Talib, was having business difficulties and Muhammad and Khadija could better provide for the child, so they took him in. Ali, who later married Muhammad's daughter Fatima, was to become one of the first converts to Islam and one of Muhammad's most fervent supporters. Muhammad also adopted another boy, a Syrian Christian named Zaid. Khadija had given him to Muhammad as a slave, but Muhammad freed the boy and he, too, became one of the first converts.

Muhammad's Wives

Khadija

On the night of the first revelation, when the archangel Gabriel had said, "Recite in the name of thy Lord," Muhammad hurried back home to Khadija, shaken and trembling. "Cover me," Muhammad said to Khadija. She rushed off and came back with his cloak and covered him. He told her what had happened and that the voice had also said, "You are the Messenger of God, and I am Gabriel."

Khadija supported Muhammad and accepted the truth of his revelations without question. Muhammad, in turn, had a great deal of respect for her and took no other wives during her lifetime. Khadija died three years before the Hijra, the migration to Medina.

After Khadija

In the twelve years between Khadija's death and Muhammad's own death, he

AISHA, MOTHER OF THE BELIEVERS

Aisha was the third of the Prophet's wives. We have much to help us picture her because there are many stories about her and sayings attributed to her preserved in hadith and the earliest biographies. Aisha was born about 614, and she grew up not remembering a time before her parents were Muslims. Her father was Abu Bakr, one of the first converts to Islam, and her mother, too, was an early convert. Muhammad was a frequent visitor to their home, often coming to consult with Abu Bakr, who was a trusted adviser.

Aisha was betrothed to the Prophet when she was still a young girl, and when she went to join his household as his wife, she quickly became the favorite. She was known for her fire and assertiveness. According to a hadith related by Aisha, the Prophet prayed in her presence and he received a revelation while he was with her, something that happened with none of his other wives. Muhammad died in her arms and was buried in her room. She was left a widow at eighteen and, as a wife of the Prophet, was forbidden to remarry. Although Aisha bore no children, she was called Mother of the Believers, a title she shared with Muhammad's other widows.

Aisha's status was further enhanced when her father, Abu Bakr, was chosen to succeed Muhammad as leader of the community. Her father, it seems, regarded her as the most able of his children. When he died, barely two years after Muhammad, he entrusted her with fulfilling his last wishes and taking care of her brothers and sisters.

Aisha continued to be outspoken and an active political force. She was apparently involved in the attempt to overthrow the third caliph, Uthman, and also tried to undermine Ali, the fourth caliph. She held a grudge against Ali, dating from a time when Muhammad was still alive and she had been accused of wrongdoing. Ali had not taken her side, and she never forgave him. When he was proclaimed the fourth caliph, Aisha joined with two of his rivals in refusing to acknowledge him. She herself took part in a battle against Ali's forces outside Basra in 656. This was the Battle of the Camel, named for Aisha's camel, from which she directed combatants and around which her supporters rallied. Ali and his supporters were victorious. Aisha was captured, but treated with dignity and respect, and taken back to Medina, where she lived out her life removed from political power.

married twelve women, including two Jewish women. All except Aisha, the daughter of Abu Bakr, had been married before. Several had become widows when their husbands died defending Islam.

It is important to remember that in Muhammad's day a man could marry more than one woman at a time. In the early years of Islam many men were killed in battle. Unless the remaining men were allowed to have more than one wife, many women would have been without husbands. Muhammad's own marriages often served to strengthen political ties at a time when the support of various tribes was essential to the survival of the religion.

Muhammad treated his wives kindly and with respect and urged others to do so, too. He said, as recorded in a hadith: "The most perfect in faith among believers is he who is the best in character and the kindest to his wives." Muhammad helped with the housework and is said to have mended his own cloak. He set the example of consulting his daughters on the question of whom they would marry, rather than simply arranging their marriages without asking them.

Islam and Women

In some ways Islam improved the status of women. It allowed them to inherit and to control their own wealth, which they had not been able to do previously. Before Islam men were not limited in the number of wives they could have. Islam limited a man to four wives and required that he treat them all equally. Some believers feel that no human being can treat four wives equally, and they interpret the Koran to mean that a man should have only one wife.

The Koran says that women should dress modestly. As we have seen, by the time Islam appeared, women in Byzantine and Persian society were veiled and secluded. These practices were adopted by Muslims and came to be associated with Islam. Over the centuries dressing modestly has been taken to mean different things in different Muslim societies.

Some take this hadith as guidance:

Aisha reported that Asma, a daughter of Abu Bakr, came to the Messenger of God—peace and blessings of God be upon him—and she was dressed in a garment made of thin cloth. The Messenger of God—peace and blessings of God be upon him—turned away from her and said: "Asma, once a woman reaches puberty, it is not proper that any part of her body be seen except this and this."

And he pointed to his face and his hands.

A group of modern Moroccan women wear one style of traditional dress: a long hooded robe with a veil that covers all but the eyes. In other parts of Morocco, women wear different traditional styles—some very colorful and bright—or they dress in Western fashions.

Basing their actions on this hadith, many women in the Muslim world wear scarves and long dresses, leaving only their faces and hands uncovered. Some Muslim women cover themselves completely, veiling their faces, too, while others feel that modest dress does not require any sort of veil or head covering.

CHAPTER FOUR

A VISION OF BEAUTY

Poetry before Islam

In pre-Islamic Arabia, the well-chosen, eloquent word was a powerful in[…]ment. In the harsh, unforgiving desert, the nomads had little in the w[…] material comforts. They did not have the means or the materials to c[…] sculpture or paintings. Instead their artistic impulses found expressi[…] poetry, the most portable of art forms, one that requires nothing other[…] well-honed senses, with which to experience the world, and memory. P[…] was composed and recited, passed down by word of mouth from gener[…] to generation.

In pre-Islamic times, poetry was already a well developed art, sophisticated meters and patterns of rhyme. Many of the ancient odes we[…] highly valued that they endured in memory for genera[…] and were finally preserved in written form in the first[…] or three centuries after the coming of Islam.

This young Bedouin from Morocco learns to read and write using the Koran for a textbook, as Muslims have done for centuries.

The Koran as the Word

When Muhammad began speaking the words of re[…] tion, his audience was already attuned to and respe[…] of the power of the word. Muhammad's revelations[…] phrased in the most moving and eloquent language an[…] had ever heard, rich in repetition, elegant turns of ph[…] and compelling rhythm. To believers, the Koran itsel[…] miracle, and its language represents the perfection o[…] Arabic language.

People of the Book

To Muslims the Koran is the Mother of Books, a[…] comes in Arabic as God's final word to humankind[…] God had already spoken to the Jews and given them a[…] and to the Christians and given them a book. In Islam[…] and Christians have a special status as People of the B[…]

people whom God had favored with revealed books, now superseded by the Koran.

The People of the Book—who came to include Zoroastrians and others—were allowed freedom to practice their religions so long as they paid their taxes and accepted the authority of their Muslim rulers. In matters of personal conduct, such as marriage, divorce, and inheritance, non-Muslims were generally bound by the laws of their own communities.

Learning and Islam

Early education was directed toward providing students with the tools they would need in the practice of their religion. Elementary education began in a school either connected with or actually in a mosque. Students would learn reading and writing with the Koran as text. The goal was to teach children what they would need to know in order to be good Muslims, and to this end girls, too, were permitted to attend elementary school. Memorization was the basic tool of learning; it was not uncommon for children of ten or so to have memorized the entire Koran. In addition to the Koran and hadith, students learned basic arithmetic, Arabic grammar, and poetry.

Schoolgirls in Malaysia learn the proper way of saying their prayers.

AL-JAHIZ

Al-Jahiz (al-JA-hiz) is one of the best known of the Abbasid writers, and his works are studied to this day as a model of elegant prose. He was born in humble circumstances in Basra, in what is now Iraq, around 776. His forebears were probably of African descent. The name al-Jahiz is actually a nickname that means "pop-eyed," referring to his bulging eyes, possibly the result of an eye disease.

Al-Jahiz had little formal education beyond Koran school, but he attended lectures at mosques and other public places, and spent time in intellectual circles that were springing up all over Basra. He was an independent and restless man who read everything he could find and mixed with all sorts of people, from the great intellectuals of his day to artisans, sailors, and even criminals.

Among al-Jahiz's best-known works is *The Book of Misers*, a collection of amusing stories about stingy people, including some leading figures of his day. Another major work, *The Book of Animals*, provides poetry and amusing anecdotes about animals, information on physiology and animal psychology, and observations on animal evolution.

Al-Jahiz witnessed the enormous changes brought about by the introduction of paper to the Muslim world in the mid-eighth century. With paper, books became inexpensive and widely available. In this passage from *The Book of Animals*, al-Jahiz sings the praises of books:

> *I can think of no item so new, born so recently, yet modest in price and easily obtained, that brings together so much excellent advice, so much rare knowledge, so many works by great minds and keen brains, so many lofty thoughts and sound ideas, so much wisdom and so much information about ancient times, distant lands, popular sayings and ruined empires, as a book.*
>
> *. . .*
>
> *A book is a companion that does not flatter you or irritate you, a chum of whom you never tire, a friend who does not fawn over you, cheat you or deceive you. . . . You will find more knowledge in one book in a month than you would find from men's mouths in five years. A book saves you the expense and trouble you get when you put yourself at the mercy of a quack teacher, inferior to you in moral qualities and in birth, and it rescues you from having to associate with obnoxious and stupid people.*
>
> *A book obeys you morning and night, at home and away from home; it needs no sleep, and it does not tire from staying up late with you. A book is a teacher that does not fail you and does not stop teaching you when you stop paying. . . . If your fortunes change, a book does not desert you, and if a fair wind blows for your enemies, a book does not turn against you. With a book as a friend, you will be able to do without everything else. You will not find yourself driven to bad company by boredom or loneliness.*

According to legend, al-Jahiz met his death smothered under an avalanche of books.

A student could continue his or her education in various settings. Girls who were continuing their studies would generally be tutored at home. Higher education was carried out informally, with scholars speaking on their works to groups gathered at the mosque or at private homes. Girls and women were sometimes brought to these lectures.

The first large-scale institution of higher education was the Bayt al-Hikma, discussed in Chapter Two. A bit later we see the forerunner of the modern universities, the Nizamiya, which was primarily a school for advanced religious study, founded in 1065–1067, also in Baghdad.

Cultural life apart from the study of religious subjects was vibrant and exciting. Educated people gathered in homes to discuss or listen to poetry or other types of literature. Several of the early caliphs sponsored poetry contests, religious debates, and literary conferences.

Libraries Flourish

Libraries were an important resource for scholars and students, and mosques often held great collections of religious books. There were also private collections and public libraries where people could borrow books. Accounts from travelers, historians, and scholars describe many important libraries flourishing by the middle of the tenth century. There was a library where students were supplied with free paper and one that paid living expenses for students working there. In some libraries books were arranged in cases and listed in catalogs, with a staff of librarians available to assist. One library in Persia was said to have housed over four hundred camel-loads of manuscripts, the titles of which filled a ten-volume catalog.

The widespread manufacture of paper was a crucial factor in the proliferation of libraries and booksellers and the general availability of books. Paper was inexpensive compared to parchment and papyrus, the primary writing materials before the introduction of paper. Technology for making paper from flax, linen, or hemp rags was brought from China around 751.

Islamic Art

Islamic culture gave rise to art forms that were and are different from those of any other art tradition. Certain features identify a work of art as Islamic—whether it be a building, a book, a ceramic piece, or a textile—whether it was produced in Malaysia or in Mali. The Taj Mahal in India is as identifiably

The Taj Mahal was built in India in the seventeenth century by the emperor Shah Jihan as a tomb for his favorite wife, Mumtaz Mahal. The domes, the towers, the beautiful garden with the reflecting pool, and the intricate arabesque designs which decorate the building combine to make this an outstanding example of Islamic architecture.

Islamic as the Alhambra in Spain. Many of the features of Islamic art were refined during the Golden Age. These features are still the basic elements by which we recognize Islamic art that is produced even today.

A common misconception is that Islam does not allow the depiction of living creatures. Actually the Koran itself says nothing about this beyond forbidding the worship of idols. There are hadith, though, that suggest that in creating pictures, the artist tries to take on God's role as creator. One hadith warns that on Judgment Day artists who create these images will be punished by being held to the impossible task of breathing life into their works.

Given these pronouncements, Islamic religious art never developed along the lines of Christian art. Islamic art has nothing like the medieval

Christian portraits of the saints, and it developed no religious sculpture. But art depicting living creatures appeared in nonreligious works, as in palace decoration, in ornamental objects, and in the well-known Persian miniatures. Persian miniatures are elaborate, highly detailed paintings used to illustrate books, often epic tales of love and heroism. This sort of painting, examples of which date from as early as the late twelfth century, reflects techniques and models seen in pre-Islamic Persian art. The finest miniatures are distinguished by their jewel-like colors and the shimmer of gold and silver. Some of the best date from the sixteenth century and were produced in what is now Iran.

Architecture

In Islamic architecture, the focus is usually on the interior of the building, not the exterior. The outside gives little clue as to what might be inside. From

This room once stood in the home of an upper-class family in Damascus. Here guests were greeted and entertained in elegance and comfort. Although the room dates from the eighteenth century, it looks very much as the home of a wealthy family in Abbasid times might have looked.

the street, one might see only high, windowless walls, but when the door is opened, a courtyard and a fountain with small trees around it might appear. Along the sides of the courtyard, rooms open up, rooms that might be decorated with beautiful mosaics, inlaid work and carved wooden window screens. Even large buildings such as mosques can be "hidden" behind plain walls and among other buildings. Many of the major mosques built during the Golden Age across the Muslim world give little indication from the outside of the size and design of the interior, or of the fine craftsmanship and elaborate detail inside.

Calligraphy

Calligraphy—beautiful writing—is probably the most characteristic Islamic art form. It grew directly from the importance of the Koran. As the word of God, the Koran was to be copied in the most elegant and beautiful script possible. Indeed, throughout the Muslim world calligraphy has always been considered the highest art.

Calligraphy was often used to decorate mosques, usually with lines from the Koran. Calligraphy was also used to create magnificent Korans. Copying the Koran or phrases from the Koran in elegant lettering was thought to bring special blessings. Some pious calligraphers would save all

The Koran should be written in a style that is beautiful but also very clear, so that someone reading it cannot misread any of the words. In the Koran pictured here, the words of the scripture are the lines in dark print in the boxes in the middle of the pages. The words in lighter print between the lines and in the margins explain the text.

This page from a Koran was copied in early Abbasid times, in the ninth century. The line across the middle of the page is done in gold. The red dots, which help the reader distinguish between similar letters, were probably added later. Arabic is written from right to left.

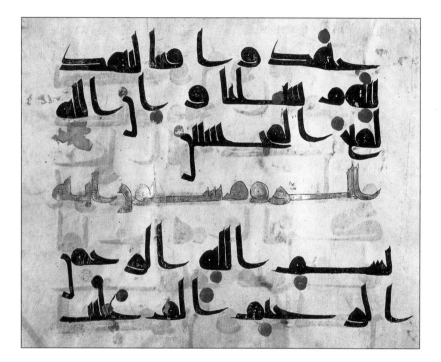

of the reed pens they had used in their lifetimes in copying the Koran so that they could be used as kindling to heat the water to wash their bodies before burial.

A knowledge of the basics of good handwriting was essential for an educated Muslim. To become a calligrapher, though, much more study was required. The student would work for years with a master calligrapher in order to obtain a license to practice the art. Women as well as men became famous calligraphers. One of the Prophet's wives was known for her beautiful writing. In later years princesses and other women of royal blood, as well as slave women and scribes, attained fame as master calligraphers.

Calligraphic art was extended to every imaginable kind of decoration. Lines of poetry might be inscribed on a cup or around the edge of a bowl or even on the blade of a sword. Not only the Koran but also secular texts—books that had nothing to do with religion—were written in painstaking calligraphy. These manuscripts were sometimes further enhanced with elaborate miniature paintings. Such books were very expensive and avidly sought by collectors. The art of calligraphy was also highly developed in other languages that came to be written in Arabic script, including Persian, Turkish, and Urdu.

The Dome of the Rock in Jerusalem, built about 691 by an Umayyad caliph, is the earliest example of calligraphy used to decorate a mosque. The rock is a holy site for Muslims, as it is thought to be where Muhammad placed his foot as he began his miraculous journey to heaven.

This area in Jerusalem is also the holiest site for Jews. The rock is thought to be the place where Abraham prepared to sacrifice his son Isaac, and it is also where the Holy of Holies of the Temple of Solomon stood. After the destruction of the Temple, the site was unoccupied until the mosque was built. During the Crusades, the mosque was used as a Christian church.

Arabesque

The arabesque is a pattern based on a design of abstract leaves or flowers radiating out, twisting back upon themselves and out again. The intricate intertwining fills the space and creates a complex design. The endless repetition and the relation of each part to the whole makes one think of the infinite. What could be more appropriate for decorating mosques and Korans than this design that mirrors the infinite nature of God?

Similar to the arabesque are repeating geometric designs, also very characteristic of Islamic art. These complex designs were created using tools no more sophisticated than a ruler and a compass. Squares and triangles could be drawn inside a circle or around its circumference, and these shapes could be further divided to form any number of one-of-a-kind designs. The designs were felt to suggest the inherent logic and order of God's universe. They create a whole by repeating a design over and over, drawing a picture of infinity.

The interior of the Dome of the Rock is decorated with arabesques. Notice the calligraphy in the blocks and circles along the lower edges of the dome. The calligraphy in the strip near the center of the dome is so elaborately done that it almost looks like an arabesque itself.

CHAPTER FIVE

THE GOLDEN AGE AND THE WORLD OF TODAY

I n 1258 Mongol hordes led by Hulegu, grandson of Ghengis Khan, pillaged and burned Baghdad. The Abbasid caliphate was finished—the caliph and his family were slaughtered—and Baghdad lay in rubble, but the light of civilization that had flourished there still shone brightly across the world it had touched.

While the Abbasids had ruled Baghdad, other cities were flourishing across the Muslim world. Despite political boundaries, scholars, artists, merchants, and travelers communicated with and influenced one another across this wide expanse. The Muslim world was also in touch with the lands beyond its borders and was very much a part of Western consciousness, as exemplified by the exchange between Harun al-Rashid and Charlemagne described at the beginning of this book.

Throughout the Golden Age the Muslim world had frequent and sometimes sustained contact with Europe and Europeans, leaving a lasting mark

The people of Baghdad look on helplessly as the Mongols storm their city.

Abd al-Rahman, the heir to the Umayyad dynasty, who had escaped the Abbasids and established an Umayyad dynasty in Spain, began building the Mosque of Cordoba in 785. The mosque was built on a site previously occupied by a Christian church, and before that by a Roman temple. Abd al-Rahman used parts of the old church, such as these Roman and Byzantine columns, but arranged them in a new and beautiful Islamic form.

on the West. Many Europeans experienced the Arab world firsthand during the period of the Crusades, from 1095 to 1270, when thousands of Europeans from all walks of life set off to reclaim Jerusalem from the Muslims. Some Europeans remained for many years in the Crusader states established in Syria, and during periods of relative peace they lived alongside Arabs. Arabic learning and culture filtered into Europe in other ways as well: through Sicily, where a Muslim dynasty ruled from the ninth to the eleventh century, and through Muslim Spain.

Muslim civilization flourished in Spain for over seven hundred years, from 710 to 1492, when Granada, the last stronghold of Muslim rule in Spain, fell to the Christian armies of Ferdinand and Isabella. During the centuries of Muslim rule there had been much contact back and forth between Spain and the rest of Europe. How Muslim Spain appeared to contemporary

Europeans is captured in the words of a Saxon nun living in the tenth century, who described Cordoba as the "jewel of the world." Like Baghdad, Cordoba boasted free schools, a university, and an important library, all of which made it an intellectual center, attracting students from Europe as well as from the Muslim world.

Crops Brought to Europe by the Arabs

One concrete way in which Arab civilization in Spain has shaped Western civilization is through the introduction of crops that have become so basic to modern life that we encounter them every day. Cotton, in Arabic *al-qutn*, was known in India and ancient Egypt but was not widely cultivated elsewhere until agricultural techniques developed by the Arabs allowed for large-scale cultivation. Cotton produced in Muslim countries was of such fine quality that it was exported to China and beyond. Cotton textiles were manufactured in Spain from the eighth century and spread to France in the twelfth century and to England a century later. The manufacture of cotton was to play an important role in the European industrial revolution.

Sugar, *al-sukkar* in Arabic, also came to the West via the Arabs, who had brought it to the Middle East from India. Egypt, Syria, and the Jordan Valley became major sugar producers and exporters. (Marco Polo tells of Egyptian technicians teaching the Chinese how to refine sugar, a rather elaborate chemical process.) Sugarcane plantations spread throughout North Africa and from there to Spain and Sicily. Western Europe, however, became acquainted with sugar through the Crusades.

Rice, *al-ruzz* in Arabic, was also introduced to Europe by the Arabs, as were sorghum, hard wheat, watermelons, eggplant, spinach, lemons, and many other fruits and vegetables. The words *scallion* and *shallot* echo the name of the Palestinian town of Ascalon, where Crusaders found them. The cultivation of many of these crops depended on irrigation, which was highly developed by the Arabs, especially in Spain. Spanish vocabulary related to canals and irrigation reflects its Arabic origins.

Paper

Paper technology, which came to Europe from the Muslim world, helped pave the way for Europe's Renaissance. By the tenth century paper mills

IBN BATTUTA: TRAVELS OF A FOURTEENTH-CENTURY ADVENTURER

In the year 1325 Ibn Battuta set out from his hometown of Tangier, in Morocco, for the holy city of Mecca. He was a man of twenty-one, educated in Muslim law. He was to spend the next thirty years of his life traveling, venturing as far as China. Along the way he worked as a judge in the Sultanate of Delhi in India, journeyed to Constantinople in the company of a Turkish princess, crossed the central Asian steppes with a caravan of yurts—the felt tents of the nomads—set upon carts and pulled by oxen, and was shipwrecked off the coast of India. He visited the Maldive Islands and Sri Lanka. Intent on seeing China, he set out again by sea, stopping along the way at Bengal, the coast of Myanmar, and the island of Sumatra, eventually arriving in Guangzhou. A few years later he returned home, stopping at Mecca for a final hajj. He visited Granada, in Spain, and then set out on his last adventure: across the Sahara by camel to the kingdom of Mali and its capital, Timbuktu.

Ibn Battuta spent his last years dictating his memoirs, and his account gives us fascinating details of life in these far-flung regions in the fourteenth century. He was interested in everything, from the price of chickens to rituals of royal ceremony to techniques of harvesting coconuts. But besides giving us glimpses into daily life across a wide expanse of the medieval world, his memoirs tell us something very basic about the world in which he lived.

Most of Ibn Battuta's travels were within the realm of Islam. The terrible Mongol conquests, which had culminated in the destruction of Baghdad in 1258, were by now a frightful memory. The Mongols, who came to rule most of Eurasia, had converted to Islam. By the time of Ibn Battuta, the Muslim world again enjoyed peace and prosperity. One could journey from the Atlantic Ocean to India and beyond—the world touched by Muslim civilization—and be assured of finding a recognizable and familiar community, united by shared beliefs and that mysterious thing we call culture.

In Cairo, Ibn Battuta stayed in this caravanserai (care-uh-VAN-su-raye). The stables were on the ground floor, and guests stayed in rooms on the upper floors.

The inlay work on these boxes, tambourines and drum, made in modern-day Egypt, continue a craft highly prized in the Middle Ages. On the tray in the center is a brass pot and small cups for Arabic coffee.

could be found in the Muslim world. Fez, in modern-day Morocco, became a noted paper-making center, and from there the technology spread to Spain. The first European paper mill was established in Italy in 1276, and in 1390 a mill was set up in Germany.

Decorative Arts

The English language to this day reflects the richness of medieval Arab crafts and decorative arts and the fact that they were admired, imported, and copied in Europe. The word *tabby* in modern English is used to describe a striped cat, but originally it referred to a certain kind of striped fabric produced in the

Attabi section of Baghdad. Damask is a kind of cloth, originally silk, with a raised pattern, named for the city of Damascus, where the finest examples of this material were produced. The silky Persian fabric *tafta*, known to us as taffeta, was brought to medieval Europe by the Arabs. *Damascene* refers to a kind of inlaid metalwork perfected in Damascus. Even the English word *sofa*— and the idea of a row of cushions for sitting—comes to us from Arabic.

Tools of Navigation and Exploration

Advances made by the Arabs in science and technology related to navigation played a direct role in European exploration. The Arabs brought the triangular lateen sail to the Mediterranean. In the fifteenth century European shipbuilders, especially the Portuguese and the Spanish, began using lateen sails along with the square sails Europeans had used since ancient times. Without this innovation, the ocean voyages of the European explorers would

The astrolabe was an essential tool for the astronomer and for the navigator, used to measure the altitudes of stars and planets. With this information, one could determine the time of day or night and one's position on the earth. Many books were written on how to build astrolabes and how to use them.

ENGLISH WORDS FROM ARABIC

Food and Crops
alfalfa
artichoke
apricot
coffee
cotton
scallion
shallot
sherbet
syrup

Naval and Trade Terms
admiral
monsoon
tariff

Textiles
mohair
muslin

Science and Mathematics
alchemy
alcohol
alkali
algebra
algorithm
sine
cipher
zero
caliber

Household
alcove
mattress
sofa
lute
ream (of paper)

Astronomy
zenith
nadir

Star Names
Aldebaran
    ("the follower")
Algenib
    ("the side")

Alhague ("the
    serpent bearer")
Algol
    ("the demon")
Rigel
    ("the leg" [of
    Orion])
Mintaka
    ("the belt")
Saiph
    ("the sword")
Betelgeuse
    ("the hand"
    [of Orion])

have been impossible, since only with the lateen sail can a ship advance against the wind. The compass, an essential instrument for long ocean voyages, had been used for navigation by Arab sailors in the eleventh century and was adopted by the Italians and used during the Crusades.

The idea that the earth was round was an ancient notion that Arab geographical works had kept alive. This theory found its way to a Latin work published in 1410, on which Columbus based his voyages.

The Legacy

Islamic civilization was a bridge across both space and time. It brought the cultures of the East—China, India, and Persia—to the West. Across time, it took the classical Western works, mainly those of the Greeks, transformed and preserved them, and passed them on to Europe. Along the way Islamic civilization added its own original ideas and put its own unique stamp on all it touched.

The Abbasid Empire died in 1258, but other great Muslim empires were to follow, among them those of the Mongols, who came to control the largest expanse of territory of any empire the world has ever seen, and the Ottomans. Emerging around 1299, the Ottomans presented a major challenge to the growing European powers for many centuries. It was only in 1683 that the tide began to turn, when the last Ottoman siege of Vienna was broken.

Muslims in Malaysia pray facing Mecca, saying the same prayers said by Muslims throughout the world.

While the Ottoman Empire weakened, European powers were expanding and establishing colonies all over the world. In the nineteenth century the French and the British gained control of most of North Africa. During World War I, the Ottoman Empire sided with the Germans, against the French and the British. The Germans lost the war, leaving the French and the British to carve up the Ottoman Empire, drawing many of the national boundaries that exist in the Middle East today. They kept some countries under their direct control and put others under the rule of political allies.

Islam Today

Many countries in the Middle East were controlled by foreign powers until quite recently, and the struggle against Western domination is still a fresh memory. Against this bitter history of colonialism, the Middle East—and other Muslim countries outside the Middle East—have struggled with poverty, overpopulation and, in some cases, unjust rulers. In response to these overwhelming obstacles, some Muslims have regarded the West as the problem and looked to their religion as a solution.

Some Muslims preach extreme ideas and say that these ideas are justified by their religion. Religious extremism is not unique to Islam. Throughout history, extremists have claimed to speak in the name of many religions—Christianity, Judaism, Hinduism, to name a few. Although the brand of Islam which appears in the headlines is often that of extremists, the majority of the world's Muslims are no more extremists than are the majority of Christians.

Islam has remained a vibrant and relevant religion, with more than a billion followers worldwide. It spread to all the lands where Arabs traded and traveled—to China, Africa and beyond—lands very different from the Arabian Peninsula which gave birth to it. The country that today accounts for the largest population of Muslims, Indonesia, is not even in the Middle East. In the United States as well as in Europe, Islam is a rapidly growing religion.

Muslim societies across the world today show commonality in basic cultural values and beliefs but also a seemingly endless variation. Just as in Abbasid times, Muslim society has taken different forms in different parts of the world, molded by the history and unique features of the society in which it has been planted, but always drawing upon its rich heritage. The Muslim culture that came to full flower in the Golden Age is very much alive today and all of us share in the gifts of its legacy.

The Golden Age of Islam: A Chronology

570 C.E.   **Birth of Muhammad**
622   **Hijra** - Muhammad and his followers flee from Mecca to Medina
    Start of Islamic calendar
630   Conquest of Mecca
632   Death of Muhammad

Muhammad's Successors: The First Caliphs
632-634   Abu Bakr governs from Medina
634-644   Umar governs from Medina
644-656   Uthman governs from Medina
656-661   Ali governs from Kufa

661-750   **Umayyad Dynasty**
    Capital: Damascus

750-1258   **Abbasid Dynasty**
    Capital: Baghdad
Early Abbasid Caliphs
750-754   Abu al-Abbas
754-775   Al-Mansur, founder of Baghdad
775-785   Al-Mahdi
785-786   Al-Hadi
786-809   **Harun Al-Rashid**
809-813   Al-Amin
813-833   Al-Mamun
945   The Buyids, a powerful Persian family, take control of Baghdad.
    They allow the Abbasids to stay, but from this time on, the Abbasids
    have little real power.
1055   Turkish tribes called Seljuks arrive in Baghdad and take   control of
    the caliphate.
1258   **The Mongols destroy Baghdad. End of the Abbasid dynasty.**

1095-1270   **The Crusades.** European Christians try to reclaim Jerusalem from the Muslims.

14th century   Ottomans appear in Anatolia
1453   Ottomans capture Constantinople
    End of Byzantine Empire. Constantinople becomes Ottoman capital, Istanbul.

1492   **Fall of Granada. End of Muslim rule in Spain**

1798   **Napoleon occupies Egypt and European colonizing of the Middle East begins.**
    1830   French rule in Algeria
    1881   French rule in Tunisia
    1882   British rule in Egypt
    1912   Italian rule in Libya
1917   Balfour Declaration issued, stating Britian's support for establishing a Jewish
    homeland in Palestine.
1920-22   In the aftermath of World War I, British and French divide up the Middle East,
    establishing most of the national boundaries as they exist today.

GLOSSARY

Abbasids (uh-BAS-ids): The Muslim dynasty that ruled from 750–1258 from its capital in Baghdad. The Abbasids traced their lineage back to Abbas, an uncle of the prophet Muhammad. Harun al-Rashid was the fifth Abbasid caliph.

arabesque: an abstract, intricate pattern of intertwining leaves or flowers

Bedouin: desert Arabs; nomads—that is, people who move from place to place, searching for grazing for their livestock

caliph (KAY-lif): literally, "successor." Caliphs were the leaders of the Muslim community after Muhammad.

caravan: a group of travelers, merchants, or pilgrims traveling together for reasons of safety

dynasty: a series of rulers who are members of the same family

calligraphy: ornamental writing

hadith (huh-DEETH): sayings or actions of the prophet Muhammad as related by his close associates and companions

hajj (hahj): pilgrimage to the city of Mecca and the holy places of Islam; a religious duty for Muslims

hijra (HEJ-ra): the migration of Muhammad and his followers from Mecca to Medina in 622 C. E. This event marks the beginning of the Islamic calendar.

jizya (JIZ-ya): a poll tax or head tax, which non-Muslim subjects paid to their Muslim rulers

Kaaba: the square building in Mecca toward which Muslims pray. Many of the rituals of the hajj, or pilgrimage, take place around the Kaaba. It is said to have been built by the Prophet Abraham and his son Ishmael.

Koran: The Muslim holy book

mosque: a Muslim place of worship

nomads: herders who follow their animals from place to place in search of food

oasis: a place in the desert that has a water supply

polytheistic: believing in more than one god

Ramadan: the Muslim month of fasting from sunrise to sunset each day

Sasanids: the dynasty that ruled in Persia from 226 C. E. until the middle of the seventh century, when it was conquered by Muslim armies

Semites: Jews, Arabs, and some other groups, all of whom speak closely related languages and belong to closely related ethnic groups

Sharia (sha-REE-a)**:** Islamic law

Umayyads (oo-MY-yads)**:** the Muslim dynasty that ruled from Damascus 661–750 C. E.

venerate: to consider sacred

zakat: a contribution of money Muslims are required to make, used for the poor and for the general good of the community

FOR FURTHER READING

Titles marked by an asterisk were written specifically for young readers.

Arberry, A. J. *The Koran Interpreted.* New York: Macmillan, 1969.

Armstrong, Karen. *Muhammad: A Biography of the Prophet.* New York: HarperSanFrancisco, 1993.

*Child, John. *The Rise of Islam.* New York: Peter Bedrick, 1993.

Dunn, Ross E. *The Adventures of Ibn Battuta: A Muslim Traveler of the Fourteenth Century.* Berkeley: University of California Press, 1989.

Fernea, Elizabeth Warnock, and Basima Qattan Bezirgan, eds. *Middle Eastern Muslim Women Speak.* Austin: University of Texas Press, 1988.

al-Hassan, Ahmad Y., and Donald R. Hill. *Islamic Technology: An Illustrated History.* Cambridge: Cambridge University Press, 1992.

Hitti, Philip K. *The Arabs: A Short History.* Chicago: Gateway Editions, 1985.

Hitti, Philip K., trans. *An Arab-Syrian Gentleman and Warrior in the Period of the Crusades: Memoirs of Usamah Ibn-Munqidh*. Princeton: Princeton University Press, 1987.

Ibn Khaldun. *The Muqaddimah: An Introduction to History*. Translated by Franz Rosenthal. Princeton: Princeton University Press, 1969.

Maalouf, Amin. *The Crusades through Arab Eyes*. New York: Schocken, 1984.

*Macdonald, Fiona. *A Sixteenth Century Mosque*. New York: Peter Bedrick, 1994.

*Mantin, Peter, and Ruth Mantin. *The Islamic World: Beliefs and Civilisations; 600–1600*. Cambridge: Cambridge University Press, 1993.

*Moktefi, Mokhtar. *The Arabs in the Golden Age*. Brookfield, Connecticut: The Millbrook Press, 1992.

Musallam, Basim. *The Arabs: A Living History*. London: Collins/Harvill, 1983.

BIBLIOGRAPHY

Abbot, Nabia. *Two Queens of Baghdad*. London: Al Saqi Books, 1986.

_____. *Aishah, the Beloved of Mohammed*. Chicago: University of Chicago Press, 1944.

Ahmed, Leila. *Women and Gender in Islam*. New Haven: Yale University Press, 1992.

Atiyeh, George N., ed. *The Book in the Islamic World: The Written Word and Communication in the Middle East*. Albany: State University of New York Press, 1995.

Ettinghausen, Richard, and Oleg Grabar. *The Art and Architecture of Islam; 650–1250*. Yale University Press, 1994.

Grabar, Oleg. *The Formation of Islamic Art*. New Haven: Yale University Press, 1987.

Hamori, A. "Love Poetry (*Ghazal*)." In *Abbasid Belles-Lettres*, edited by Julia Ashtiany et al. Cambridge: Cambridge University Press, 1990.

Hayes, John R., ed. *The Genius of Arab Civilization: Source of Renaissance.* Cambridge: The MIT Press, 1983.

Hitti, Philip K. *History of the Arabs*, 10th Edition. New York: St. Martin's Press, 1985.

Hodgson, Marshall G. S. *The Venture of Islam.* 3 vols. Chicago: University of Chicago Press, 1977.

Hourani, Albert. *A History of the Arab Peoples.* Cambridge, Massachusetts: Harvard University Press, 1991.

Komaroff, Linda. *Islamic Art in the Metropolitan Museum: The Historical Context.* New York: The Metropolitan Museum of Art, 1992.

Lapidus, Ira M. *A History of Islamic Societies.* Cambridge: Cambridge University Press, 1995.

Lings, Martin. *Muhammad: His Life Based on the Earliest Sources.* Rochester, Vermont: Inner Traditions, 1983.

Mitchell, George, ed. *Architecture of the Islamic World: Its History and Social Meaning.* London: Thames and Hudson, 1991.

Nashat, Guity. "Women in the Middle East; 8,000 B. C.–A. D. 1800." In *Restoring Women to History.* Bloomington: Organization of American Historians, 1988.

Pellat, C. "Al-Jahiz." In *Abbasid Belles-Lettres*, edited by Julia Ashtiany. Cambridge: Cambridge University Press, 1990.

Peters, F. E. *Judaism, Christianity, and Islam: The Classical Texts and Their Interpretation.* Princeton: Princeton University Press, 1990.

_____. *The Hajj: The Muslim Pilgrimage to Mecca and the Holy Places.* Princeton: Princeton University Press, 1994.

Saliba, George. *A History of Arabic Astronomy: Planetary Theories During the Golden Age of Islam.* New York: New York University Press, 1994.

Schimmel, Annemarie. *Calligraphy and Islamic Culture.* New York: New York University Press, 1990.

Young, M. J. L., J. D. Latham, and R. B. Serjeant. *Religion, Learning and Science in the Abbasid Period.* Cambridge: Cambridge University Press, 1990.

INDEX

Page numbers for illustrations are in boldface

ABOUT THE AUTHOR

"I first visited the Middle East many years ago as a college student and I have been fascinated by it ever since. I am enthralled by the beauty of Arabic calligraphy, which you see everywhere in the Middle East, and by the music of the spoken language. I love reading medieval Arabic texts—literature, histories, accounts of travelers, biographies—windows into an intriguing world."

Linda George has a Ph.D. in linguistics from Harvard University. She wrote her doctoral dissertation on language change and storytelling, based on a 14th century Arabic manuscript of *The Thousand and One Nights.* She has lived in Egypt and Morocco and has worked in and visited many other parts of the Arab world. She has taught Middle East history and literature at Columbia University in New York and at Drew University in Madison, New Jersey.

She lives in New Jersey with her husband, Richard, and their son, Alexander.